31 Days In Proverbs!

31 Days In
PROVERBS!

Living A Life Filled With Wisdom

Joy Nicole Smith

XULON PRESS

Xulon Press
2301 Lucien Way #415
Maitland, FL 32751
407.339.4217
www.xulonpress.com

Unless otherwise indicated, Scripture quotations taken from the King James
Version (KJV) – *public domain*.

Scripture quotations taken from the Holy Bible, New Living Translation
(NLT). Copyright ©1996, 2004, 2007 by Tyndale House Foundation. Used
by permission of Tyndale House Publishers, Inc.

Paperback ISBN-13: 978-1-66287-946-3
Ebook ISBN-13: 978-1-66287-947-0

Wisdom, knowledge, and understanding all seem to work together for the greater good of humanity.

I began this 31-day fast not only to be wiser but for God to pour out His discernment and understanding upon me. As a church leader, I need to be able to see physically, spiritually, and with clarity to lead God's people. I want to obtain, retain, and manage God's resources properly and have the ability to multiply these things exponentially. With all of this in mind, I thought I should be in contact with the greatest teachers to lead and guide me on this journey. So here we are in the book of Proverbs, known to be written by the wisest man to ever live. And I will not even begin to start this learning process without asking Jesus to pour out His holy counsel upon me which will teach, lead, reveal, and guide me along my way. I can only hope that what God has given to me over my 31 days of fasting will help you also while you are on your journey to greatness.

Table of Content
Proverbs

Day 1–Proverbs Chapter One

The Purpose of Proverbs

We are all looking for a purpose. Rather, it is the purpose of life or the purpose within ourselves. We want to know the value and reasons for things that occur in life. Now, let's get ready to research the purpose of Proverbs.

1 The proverbs of Solomon the son of David, king of Israel;

*2 To know wisdom and instruction; to perceive
the words of understanding;*

*3 To receive the instruction of wisdom, justice,
and judgment, and equity;*

*4 To give subtilty to the simple, to the young man
knowledge and discretion.*

Most of us want to live successful lives. To do so takes discipline and structure. We as people need to have guidelines on what is good, right, fair, and just. When we as people do not have a disciplined foundation, we tend to make up stuff just to fit ourselves and no one else. Look at our communities and politics. Do they show justice or what is right? Do the rules only seem to benefit some and not others? These proverbs or personal bite-size nuggets of wisdom are supposed to be simple enough for all to understand because it may take some of us a little longer to grasp concepts. And for the young people, they can learn to apply these same wise concepts to real-life situations that they may face.

5 A wise man will hear, and will increase learning;
and a man of understanding shall attain unto wise counsels:

6 To understand a proverb, and the interpretation;
the words of the wise, and their dark sayings.

The words of wisdom are designed so that when wise men and women, boys and girls hear them, they won't say, "I know that already". They will listen to them, again and again, to become even wiser! How awesome would your circle of wise friends be if they became even wiser!? Most of us, at any mature state in life, has some kind of under-standing of what is right. Oftentimes, we know right from wrong; we just want to know exactly what to do and we want to make the right decisions. These proverbs will tell us just that! The wise want to think and figure out hidden truths. Look at Jesus! He often taught in parables, for they are earthy stories with a heavenly meaning. But why, you ask? For many different reasons, like practical understanding or life applica-tion made easy, all while hiding valuable information from the foolish.

7 The fear of the Lord is the beginning of knowledge:
but fools despise wisdom and instruction.

The meaning of fear here is not to be scared of God or scared by God. It means to love God above all other people, places, things, or ideas. To have the most respect, honor, and loyalty for the most high God, the Creator of all above and below. Once you have this type of reverence for God, it is only then that you are able to start walking into true wisdom and knowledge. This is how you can begin to identify the stupid. They will lack the fear of the Lord and they will not be disciplined. They may say things like Y.O.L.O!- You Only Live Once! And their life decisions will be questionable.

> **8** *My son, hear the instruction of thy father,*
> *and forsake not the law of thy mother:*

> **9** *For they shall be an ornament of grace unto thy head,*
> *and chains about thy neck.*

In these verses, it sounds like a very concerned parent trying to prepare their child for life. This parent wants their child or children to live a life pleasing unto God. A life that is full of success and honor that the world cannot give. The word listen means more than just hearing with your ears. It means to take action after the instructions and corrections have been given. When you are actively listening, you are able to repeat, complete the action, and remember the wisdom you have been given. For those who have had any wise parenting, be it biological or not, have you not said, "I should have listened when I had the chance"? How better off would you have been if you had listened to wise counsel? When we learn from wise teaching and corrections, it's like showing off grace on top of our heads, like a fine royal crown. Grace from God is an honor. It is His power and righteousness given to us. Know that this chain is not to physically bind you. It should be shown off as a luxurious jewel, just like how most celebrities show off their big lavish gold, silver, and platinum jewelry decked out with fine diamonds.

> **10** *My son, if sinners entice thee, consent thou not.*

> **11** *If they say, Come with us, let us lay wait for blood,*
> *let us lurk privily for the innocent without cause:*

*12 Let us swallow them up alive as the grave; and whole,
as those that go down into the pit:*

*13 We shall find all precious substance,
we shall fill our houses with spoil:*

14 Cast in thy lot among us; let us all have one purse:

It is very sad in our society today where a lot of this kind of activity occurs. We see this on a vast scale with gang violence. Homicides fill the news and social media daily around the world. You hear the young people referring to "hitting licks", which is robbery. These actions are what you would call criminal activity. Pay attention to how King Solomon opens this section of Proverbs with my son. Good active parents want their children to live and act respectfully. I personally do not want my children killing others for sport or goods, and I don't want my children behind bars over criminal activity. If society as a whole followed these few proverbs, how better off would the world be? We ourselves and our children should turn away from these evil acts and those who indulge in them.

*15 My son, walk not thou in the way with them;
refrain thy foot from their path:*

16 For their feet run to evil, and make haste to shed blood.

17 Surely in vain the net is spread in the sight of any bird.

*18 And they lay wait for their own blood;
they lurk privily for their own lives.*

*19 So are the ways of every one that is greedy of gain;
which taketh away the life of the owners thereof.*

This information must be important because, yet again, our teacher repeats himself. Do not even go with those who intend to do evil. This is because the ones who go along with it are just as guilty. It reminds me of a song that says, "Don't let the devil ride, because if you let him ride, he will want to drive, and he will drive you away". Even though it seems like evil succeeds here on earth, there is an eternity that we have to consider. Either eternity in God's presence filled with His glory, or in His absence living in His eternal wrath.

20 Wisdom crieth without; she uttereth her voice in the streets:

21 She crieth in the chief place of concourse, in the openings of the gates: in the city she uttereth her words, saying,

22 How long, ye simple ones, will ye love simplicity? and the scorners delight in their scorning, and fools hate knowledge?

23 Turn you at my reproof: behold, I will pour out my spirit unto you, I will make known my words unto you.

I believe women are secret weapons. They can go places men cannot and they see things that are different from the man's perspective. They can be soft and gentle, yet strong and mighty interchangeably. She is a mass multiplier and defender of her own. She is so great because she was taken out of the man in his prime, to stand next to him as his helpmate. Wisdom calls for all to be wise, as she is willing to share her innermost self to make us wise. However, society treats wisdom just as any other woman–a woman that has been seen as weak and needing only to be seen and not heard. But oh, how much more she is worth than all the riches on this earth.

Wisdom wants us to wake up and have both understanding and knowledge. Wisdom does not want us to walk in simplemindedness, and just go with the flow. Wisdom wonders how long will they continue to be foolish, acting like idiots and hating knowledge. Why do they hate knowledge? Well, knowledge brings accountability. Once you know better, you are held accountable to do better. Let's listen to wisdom's counsel, guidance, and teachings, so God will share His heart and make us wise.

24 Because I have called, and ye refused;
I have stretched out my hand, and no man regarded;

25 But ye have set at nought all my counsel,
and would none of my reproof:

26 I also will laugh at your calamity;
I will mock when your fear cometh;

27 When your fear cometh as desolation, and your destruction
cometh as a whirlwind; when distress and anguish cometh upon you.

28 Then shall they call upon me, but I will not answer;
they shall seek me early, but they shall not find me:

29 For that they hated knowledge,
and did not choose the fear of the Lord:

30 They would none of my counsel: they despised all my reproof.

31 Therefore shall they eat of the fruit of their own way,
and be filled with their own devices.

32 For the turning away of the simple shall slay them,
and the prosperity of fools shall destroy them.

33 But whoso hearkeneth unto me shall dwell safely, and shall be quiet from fear of evil.

And here goes wisdom with her "I told you so" moment! There will be no pity because you chose to reject the right way. Once you have chosen to reject wisdom, you have rejected God. Like Adam and Eve disobeyed God's commands, they had to deal with and endure the bitter consequences of their actions. We have to deal with what comes next when we choose to live in our own ways. We end up making life so much harder for ourselves. Now there are two types of wisdom: like unto God and like unto the world. Which wisdom will you follow?

Day 2–Proverbs Chapter Two

1 My son, if thou wilt receive my words,
and hide my commandments with thee;

2 So that thou incline thine ear unto wisdom,
and apply thine heart to understanding;

3 Yea, if thou criest after knowledge,
and liftest up thy voice for understanding;

4 If thou seekest her as silver,
and searchest for her as for hid treasures;

5 Then shalt thou understand the fear of the Lord,
and find the knowledge of God.

6 For the Lord giveth wisdom: out of his mouth cometh
knowledge and understanding.

7 He layeth up sound wisdom for the righteous:
he is a buckler to them that walk uprightly.

8 He keepeth the paths of judgment, and preserveth
the way of his saints.

Again, we are being guided as children, by our loving parents who want us to do our best in this life. We are told not only to hear wisdom but to listen to wisdom as well. Here are our instructions, and we are advised to ask questions if we do not understand something. Ask questions that will lead you to understand the concepts and truths. Don't just sit and be confused. If getting your question answered will lead you to knowledge and understanding, ask away! Wisdom is worth more than hidden treasures. That is why we are instructed to search, dig, and ask for wisdom. If you want good valuable wisdom, you must obtain it from God. But remember, you must first reverence and fear God.

9 Then shalt thou understand righteousness, and judgment, and equity; yea, every good path.

10 When wisdom entereth into thine heart, and knowledge is pleasant unto thy soul;

11 Discretion shall preserve thee, understanding shall keep thee:

Now, this is referring to the choices and decisions that we make in this life. Acknowledged that if we are in Christ, then the world will hate us, just as the world hates what is right. Wisdom will not free us from the trials and tribulations that we will experience, just as it did not for Job. However, God protects and provides for His own. He restored all that was taken from Job, and He gives a peace that surpasses all understanding. That's why wise choices will watch over you and understanding will keep you.

12 To deliver thee from the way of the evil man, from the man that speaketh froward things;

13 Who leave the paths of uprightness, t
o walk in the ways of darkness;

14 Who rejoice to do evil, and delight in the
frowardness of the wicked;

15 Whose ways are crooked, and they froward in their paths:

16 To deliver thee from the strange woman,
even from the stranger which flattereth with her words;

17 Which forsaketh the guide of her youth,
and forgetteth the covenant of her God.

18 For her house inclineth unto death, and her paths unto the dead.

19 None that go unto her return again, neither take they
hold of the paths of life.

Wisdom will help you choose wise friends and steer you away from manipulative people. Wisdom will also help you in choosing a wise helpmate. The proverb instructions were initially given to a son, from a father's perspective, teaching him how a wise woman will do a man well as his helpmate.

Now let's look at the spiritual meaning of this wise woman. She is wisdom which leads to the path that is pleasing to God. Her home is a destination of unimaginable good things. There is also the wicked woman who pleases the world, leading to the wrath of God and resulting in no good thing.

20 That thou mayest walk in the way of good men, and keep the
paths of the righteous.

21 *For the upright shall dwell in the land,*
and the perfect shall remain in it.

22 *But the wicked shall be cut off from the earth,*
and the transgressors shall be rooted out of it.

When your circle is full of good and wise people, we, as members of the group, tend to do good and wise things. However, when our circle is full of foolish and worldly people, we likewise tend to do foolish and worldly things. You know, the whole birds of a feather flock together. God often had land set aside for His people to reside in. His people were driven out of their God-given land because of their rejection and disobedience toward Him. Let's look at this as being in the heavenly realm, where the wicked are not welcomed, and the treacherous are uprooted from the presence of God. Only those with integrity will remain in the land. Where you reside will depend on your wise or foolish decisions.

Day 3–Proverbs Chapter Three

1 My son, forget not my law;
but let thine heart keep my commandments:

2 For length of days, and long life, and peace, shall they add to thee.

3 Let not mercy and truth forsake thee: bind them about thy neck;
write them upon the table of thine heart:

4 So shalt thou find favour and good understanding i
n the sight of God and man.

By day 3, we should see the importance of listening and remembering what we are being taught by King Solomon. Honoring your father and mother is part of the ten commandments as well. Honoring our parents' lengthens our days. Of course, we want to live long and satisfying lives. Now we know how this type of life is obtained. When we honor, obey, and follow wise instructions, it makes life easier. Two things we need to keep with us are loyalty and kindness. These attributes should be deep within our character. The benefit of having the two is favor with God and man. So, what is favor? Favor is when you have approval and support. That has to feel amazing to have favor from both God and man. We need to keep loyalty and kindness deep in our hearts. Okay, what is loyalty and kindness? Loyalty is faithfulness, the act and the mindset of being committed. And kindness is to be gentle, concerned, thoughtful, unselfish, compassionate, generous, merciful, etc. This is how you earn a magnificent reputation.

5 *Trust in the LORD with all thine heart;*
and lean not unto thine own understanding.

6 *In all thy ways acknowledge him, and he shall direct thy paths.*

Now that we live with loyalty and kindness, trust in God with your whole heart. Even when it looks like we can figure it out on our own, it is best to consult the Lord our God first. That way He will show us which way to go. For He alone knows all possible outcomes.

7 *Be not wise in thine own eyes: fear the LORD, and depart from evil.*

8 *It shall be health to thy navel, and marrow to thy bones.*

Even when you come up with a really good idea of your own, don't allow that to amaze you. If it were not for God, that idea would not have entered your mind. So give the glory to whom it is due, and that is to God. The fear of the Lord and turning from evil comes with its own set of rewards, such as health and strength.

9 *Honour the LORD with thy substance, and with*
the firstfruits of all thine increase:

10 *So shall thy barns be filled with plenty, and thy presses*
shall burst out with new wine.

11 *My son, despise not the chastening of the LORD;*
neither be weary of his correction:

12 For whom the LORD loveth he correcteth;
even as a father the son in whom he delighteth.

When you receive your wealth, honor God with it first. Then you won't be without any good thing. Oftentimes, we get upset with God when He corrects us when actually, we should rejoice in the fact that He is showing us love. He is taking the time to correct those he loves. This, in return, should put us back on the right track, if we listen to our Father's corrections and instructions. We need repetition for memory purposes and life application. That way, we can be sure wisdom has been written on our hearts.

13 Happy is the man that findeth wisdom, and the man
that getteth understanding.

14 For the merchandise of it is better than the merchandise of silver,
and the gain thereof than fine gold.

15 She is more precious than rubies: and all the things
thou canst desire are not to be compared unto her.

16 Length of days is in her right hand; and in her
left hand riches and honour.

17 Her ways are ways of pleasantness, and all her paths are peace.

18 She is a tree of life to them that lay hold upon her:
and happy is every one that retaineth her.

For those to whom God grants wisdom and understanding, what they have is worth more than anything they could ever desire here on earth. Wisdom offers wonderful gifts in her hands. She is willing to give long life, riches, and honor. Is that not what we all desire for our lives today?

19 The LORD by wisdom hath founded the earth; by understanding hath he established the heavens.

20 By his knowledge the depths are broken up, and the clouds drop down the dew.

This wisdom, knowledge, and understanding are way deeper than what we can even fathom. God Himself used wisdom to create the earth. He used understanding to create the heavens, and with knowledge, God gives us a water cycling system. Let's all just take a moment here to say, "HOW GREAT IS OUR GOD! "

21 My son, let not them depart from thine eyes: keep sound wisdom and discretion:

22 So shall they be life unto thy soul, and grace to thy neck.

23 Then shalt thou walk in thy way safely, and thy foot shall not stumble.

24 When thou liest down, thou shalt not be afraid: yea, thou shalt lie down, and thy sleep shall be sweet.

25 Be not afraid of sudden fear, neither of the desolation of the wicked, when it cometh.

26 For the LORD shall be thy confidence, and shall keep thy foot from being taken.

I've heard my mother say many times that common sense ain't so common. And it is surely the truth! People do some unconventional things these days. So, when we are able to think clearly and analyze correctly, peace comes upon us with our decisions. We can then lay down at night with no worry because we are living wise and righteously; therefore, God will continue to keep and protect us.

> *27 Withhold not good from them to whom it is due,*
> *when it is in the power of thine hand to do it.*

> *28 Say not unto thy neighbour, Go, and come again,*
> *and tomorrow I will give; when thou hast it by thee.*

We do not want God to withhold any good thing from us. In the same manner, we shouldn't withhold any good thing from those around us. We do not have the authority to choose who deserves good things when it is in our power to help others. Likewise, our word should be our bond, when we say we will do something for someone else. We should definitely take action right away and not have someone waiting for no reason. All I am trying to say is, do what you can when you can, and do it in a timely fashion.

> *29 Devise not evil against thy neighbour,*
> *seeing he dwelleth securely by thee.*

30 Strive not with a man without cause, if he have done thee no harm.

31 Envy thou not the oppressor, and choose none of his ways.

> *32 For the froward is abomination to the LORD:*
> *but his secret is with the righteous.*

33 *The curse of the* L<small>ORD</small> *is in the house of the wicked:*
but he blesseth the habitation of the just.

34 *Surely he scorneth the scorners: but he giveth grace unto the lowly.*

35 *The wise shall inherit glory: but shame shall be*
the promotion of fools.

This part simply means to do right by others and treat them the way you would want to be treated. Don't fight with others without cause or reason. You wouldn't want people picking on you for no reason, so don't be a bully! You don't want to live the lifestyles of violent people. Copying their ways will only land you far from the presence of God. Now that's a bad idea! It's better to be called a friend of God, rather than an enemy of God. Stand in the light of God's blessings and allow God to be gracious and show favor to you and your house. Just don't be put to shame because you failed to turn to God and did not choose the ways of wisdom.

Day 4–Proverbs Chapter Four

1 Hear, ye children, the instruction of a father, and attend to know understanding.

2 For I give you good doctrine, forsake ye not my law.

3 For I was my father's son, tender and only beloved in the sight of my mother.

4 He taught me also, and said unto me, Let thine heart retain my words: keep my commandments, and live.

5 Get wisdom, get understanding: forget it not; neither decline from the words of my mouth.

6 Forsake her not, and she shall preserve thee: love her, and she shall keep thee.

7 Wisdom is the principal thing; therefore get wisdom: and with all thy getting get understanding.

8 Exalt her, and she shall promote thee: she shall bring thee to honour, when thou dost embrace her.

9 She shall give to thine head an ornament of grace: a crown of glory shall she deliver to thee.

*10 Hear, O my son, and receive my sayings;
and the years of thy life shall be many.*

*11 I have taught thee in the way of wisdom;
I have led thee in right paths.*

*12 When thou goest, thy steps shall not be straitened;
and when thou runnest, thou shalt not stumble.*

*13 Take fast hold of instruction; let her not go: keep her;
for she is thy life.*

It is so important for us to listen to our wise elders, those who have good judgment and guidance. When we study wisdom repetitively, we are able to absorb wisdom fully, ensuring that wisdom is written on our hearts. The more wisdom we have, the more likely we are to do better. This is because now we know better; therefore, we can make better choices. When you have wise teachers, pay very close attention to them. They, too, have been young once, and have made decisions that they weren't proud of. This gives them the experience to tell us how not to fall into the same obstacles that would hinder us in life. This will result in you having better success than they themselves had. When we follow wise advice and walk in wisdom, we are actually following Christ. Turning from evil may not seem like you're having a good time in your youth, but it keeps you safe from all sorts of unwanted disasters along the way.

*14 Enter not into the path of the wicked,
and go not in the way of evil men.*

15 Avoid it, pass not by it, turn from it, and pass away.

16 For they sleep not, except they have done mischief; and their sleep is taken away, unless they cause some to fall.

*17 For they eat the bread of wickedness,
and drink the wine of violence.*

18 But the path of the just is as the shining light, that shineth more and more unto the perfect day.

*19 The way of the wicked is as darkness:
they know not at what they stumble.*

20 My son, attend to my words; incline thine ear unto my sayings.

*21 Let them not depart from thine eyes; keep them in
the midst of thine heart.*

*22 For they are life unto those that find them,
and health to all their flesh.*

King Solomon is leaving this wise instruction to his children, but can't you see this as a mirror image of God leaving His instruction to all of His children? God desires for us to choose Him. He wants us to live righteously so we can live freely in His presence always. But for us to be able to do so, we must know how, so He constantly reminds us through His Holy Spirit to live wisely.

23 Keep thy heart with all diligence; for out of it are the issues of life.

*24 Put away from thee a froward mouth, and perverse lips
put far from thee.*

25 *Let thine eyes look right on, and let thine eyelids*
look straight before thee.

26 *Ponder the path of thy feet, and let all thy ways be established.*

27 *Turn not to the right hand nor to the left: remove thy foot from evil.*

Your heart is like the door or mouth to your soul. What you sense through your five senses feeds your soul. What are you feeding your soul, through what you see, hear, taste, smell, and feel? We should be protecting our hearts and souls from evil through these gateways. For example, perverse talk. If you are around someone who is always using curse words, after a while, you will notice that you will begin to use those same words in your speech, where you wouldn't have before. This is why we should avoid evil; it has a way of rubbing off on us fast! If you watch violent and sexualized things, you may become more violent and sexualized. If you drink alcohol, over time, you may need more to feel good, and your wise judgment will be altered (that goes for any drug as well). For some people, certain scents become a fetish. And when something feels good, we continue to do it over and over to satisfy what the body wants. This is why we need to protect our hearts from evil.

Once you decide to follow Christ and live righteously for God, do just that and stay focused. It is so easy to be evil. The hard work comes in when it is time to live wise and righteously. Even though it is not easy staying away from evil, the reward for evil is death. If you want the blessings and good rewards that God has for His children, stay away from evil and its path. Evil is the trap made to capture your soul for eternity, so don't get sidetracked by evil.

Day 5–Proverbs Chapter Five

1 My son, attend unto my wisdom, and bow thine ear to my understanding:

2 That thou mayest regard discretion, and that thy lips may keep knowledge.

I don't want you to feel that because King Solomon keeps speaking to his son or his children that this wisdom is not for you today. The Wisdom that is being taught is to be handed down from generation to generation so that your wise sons can become wise fathers and your wise daughters can become wise mothers. In return, they can teach and raise wise children. And if perhaps you never parent children of your own, that's okay. You can still be a wise counselor, teacher, mentor, and advisor to those you may come in contact with and build relationships with. King Solomon is reminding us to listen and pay attention to wise teachings so that we can share wisdom through our speech and our actions.

3 For the lips of a strange woman drop as an honeycomb, and her mouth is smoother than oil:

4 But her end is bitter as wormwood, sharp as a two-edged sword.

5 Her feet go down to death; her steps take hold on hell.

*6 Lest thou shouldest ponder the path of life,
her ways are moveable, that thou canst not know them.*

This portion of Proverbs is instructing us to stay away from the immoral woman. In previous chapters, wisdom was described as a woman. Now, this is not for you to look at women differently because wisdom teaches both males and females. Immorality corrupts both males and females. These illustrations are to help guide us to a better understanding, so we can apply these principles to our daily lives with ease. Jesus is wisdom, and anything that rebels against God is antichrist.

Doing evil and corrupt things seems fun at first; however, it produces God's anger. Death just seems to be easy to write off because we all will die. Nonetheless, all will not experience the bitter poison of death. There is a literal war going on right now for your soul, and you get to decide whose team you want to be on. And let me tell you, results will vary on the personal decisions you make. Proverbs is more than just learning and retaining wisdom while living a successful life; it's salvation for the soul.

*7 Hear me now therefore, O ye children, and depart
not from the words of my mouth.*

*8 Remove thy way far from her, and come not nigh
the door of her house:*

*9 Lest thou give thine honour unto others,
and thy years unto the cruel:*

*10 Lest strangers be filled with thy wealth;
and thy labours be in the house of a stranger;*

*11 And thou mourn at the last, when thy flesh
and thy body are consumed,*

*12 And say, How have I hated instruction,
and my heart despised reproof;*

*13 And have not obeyed the voice of my teachers,
nor inclined mine ear to them that instructed me!*

*14 I was almost in all evil in the midst of the
congregation and assembly.*

Stay away from her and her children! What does this mean? Stay away from whatever immoral acts are considered to go against God's commands. Okay, let me break it down: stay away from evil thoughts, sexual immorality, theft, murder, adultery, greed, wickedness, deceit, lustful desires, envy, slander, pride, foolishness, impurity, idolatry, sorcery, hostility, strife, jealousy, fits of rage, dissensions, divisions, drunkenness, orgies, and faithlessness. You know, things like these! Not falling into immoral traps will save you from public humiliation.

*15 Drink waters out of thine own cistern, and running waters
out of thine own well.*

*16 Let thy fountains be dispersed abroad,
and rivers of waters in the streets.*

17 Let them be only thine own, and not strangers' with thee.

18 Let thy fountain be blessed: and rejoice with the wife of thy youth.

19 Let her be as the loving hind and pleasant roe; let her breasts satisfy thee at all times; and be thou ravished always with her love.

If you are married, GO HOME! Don't eat, drink, sleep, fix anything, or visit a place unpleasant to God or to your spouse. Your love mentally, physically, and spiritually should stay between you, God, and your spouse! No one outside that trinity should get your love; it is not to be shared elsewhere. Not married? No problem! Keep your body to yourself. No good comes out from having sex with strangers or a bunch of people. Save yourself! There is nothing safe out in the streets! If you are married, work on producing great things in your marriage with one another like loving each other, having children, building businesses and legacies, etc. If you are not married and want to be, prepare yourself so that when the time comes you will have great things to bring to the home. This way, your home will be built on a solid godly foundation.

20 And why wilt thou, my son, be ravished with a strange woman, and embrace the bosom of a stranger?

21 For the ways of man are before the eyes of the LORD, and he pondereth all his goings.

22 His own iniquities shall take the wicked himself, and he shall be holden with the cords of his sins.

23 He shall die without instruction; and in the greatness of his folly he shall go astray.

Nobody wants what everybody else has had! God is watching and taking account of all that we have done and are doing. We need self-control in life. Self-control will help us stay committed to making wise decisions. Immortality is always there waiting to take us captive. Being captive by immortality results in God's everlasting punishment. Remember to choose wisely.

Day 6–Proverbs Chapter Six

1 My son, if thou be surety for thy friend,
if thou hast stricken thy hand with a stranger,

2 Thou art snared with the words of thy mouth,
thou art taken with the words of thy mouth.

3 Do this now, my son, and deliver thyself, when thou art come into
the hand of thy friend; go, humble thyself, and make sure thy friend.

4 Give not sleep to thine eyes, nor slumber to thine eyelids.

5 Deliver thyself as a roe from the hand of the hunter,
and as a bird from the hand of the fowler.

What a lesson on how to manage your money. Co-signing can get you into a lot of unwanted trouble. Borrowing even for yourself without a disciplined plan and financial stability is detrimental to your name. You could end up needing to file bankruptcy just so you can try and start over somehow. In this world, all you have is your name, so keep it clean. Bad Credit is terrible to have, and bill collectors calling you is even worse. Spend your money wisely.

6 Go to the ant, thou sluggard; consider her ways, and be wise:

7 Which having no guide, overseer, or ruler,

8 *Provideth her meat in the summer, and gathereth*
her food in the harvest.

9 *How long wilt thou sleep, O sluggard?*
when wilt thou arise out of thy sleep?

10 *Yet a little sleep, a little slumber,*
a little folding of the hands to sleep:

11 *So shall thy poverty come as one that travelleth,*
and thy want as an armed man.

Don't be afraid to work. Don't choose sleep over work. Poverty is real and affects many. Find work that allows you to save for rainy days and retirement. And within your home, have emergency supplies plus extra food and water. This is important for just-in-case scenarios. We have no idea how the world may turn and change from one day to the next.

12 *A naughty person, a wicked man, walketh with a froward mouth.*

13 *He winketh with his eyes, he speaketh with his feet,*
he teacheth with his fingers;

14 *Frowardness is in his heart, he deviseth mischief continually;*
he soweth discord.

15 *Therefore shall his calamity come suddenly; suddenly shall*
he be broken without remedy.

16 *These six things doth the LORD hate: yea, seven are*
an abomination unto him:

17 A proud look, a lying tongue, and hands that shed innocent blood,

18 An heart that deviseth wicked imaginations, feet that be
swift in running to mischief,

19 A false witness that speaketh lies, and he that
soweth discord among brethren.

There is no good thing that comes out of wicked liars with per-verted hearts. What benefit do you reap out of being what God hates? Do you realize the destruction we are willing to pour out on ourselves, by waging war with God through our evil acts? Listen to wisdom and choose wisely!

20 My son, keep thy father's commandment,
and forsake not the law of thy mother:

21 Bind them continually upon thine heart,
and tie them about thy neck.

22 When thou goest, it shall lead thee; when thou sleepest, it shall
keep thee; and when thou awakest, it shall talk with thee.

23 For the commandment is a lamp; and the law is light;
and reproofs of instruction are the way of life:

24 To keep thee from the evil woman, from the flattery
of the tongue of a strange woman.

25 Lust not after her beauty in thine heart;
neither let her take thee with her eyelids.

26 For by means of a whorish woman a man is brought to a piece of bread: and the adultress will hunt for the precious life.

27 Can a man take fire in his bosom, and his clothes not be burned?

28 Can one go upon hot coals, and his feet not be burned?

29 So he that goeth in to his neighbour's wife; whosoever toucheth her shall not be innocent.

30 Men do not despise a thief, if he steal to satisfy his soul when he is hungry;

31 But if he be found, he shall restore sevenfold; he shall give all the substance of his house.

32 But whoso committeth adultery with a woman lacketh understanding: he that doeth it destroyeth his own soul.

33 A wound and dishonour shall he get; and his reproach shall not be wiped away.

34 For jealousy is the rage of a man: therefore he will not spare in the day of vengeance.

35 He will not regard any ransom; neither will he rest content, though thou givest many gifts.

Only if we will listen to the wisdom being poured out on us will we be saved from an everlasting life of destruction. Keep this wisdom close. God's wisdom leads to blessings, deliverance, and longevity. In this portion of Proverbs, take everything King Solomon had said at face value in this physical world. Now it is time to apply it physically and spiritually in our lives. Spiritually, we should not pimp or prostitute ourselves to immoral living. We, as believers in Christ, both male and female, are the bride of Christ. We must live as godly and wise wives, for we have a jealous husband (God). How upset will He be when He comes home to see what we have been up to? The evil we have done will not go unpunished. So, choose wisely today whom you will serve.

Day 7–Proverbs Chapter 7

1 My son, keep my words, and lay up my commandments with thee.

*2 Keep my commandments, and live; and my law
as the apple of thine eye.*

3 Bind them upon thy fingers, write them upon the table of thine heart.

The more I learn from the teachings of King Solomon, the more I really see the wisdom of God pour out through him. God, Our Father, is giving us everything that we need to be successful and to live. Solomon asked that God would give him wisdom, knowledge, and understanding to lead His people. And pay attention to the words that Solomon uses to teach us wisdom today. It sounds just like the instructions God has given to lead us to Himself. Follow God's instructions, listen, and obey for God is literally showing us the way to Him.

*4 Say unto wisdom, Thou art my sister; and call
understanding thy kinswoman:*

*5 That they may keep thee from the strange woman,
from the stranger which flattereth with her words.*

Again, these analogies are for understanding purposes. Love wisdom like a sister. What wouldn't you do for your sister, brother, or close family member? Look further than male or female; look at the role they play in life. Ask God to open your spiritual eyes. We need to be able to see clearly both physically and spiritually; this is how we will be able to understand and discern properly. We need God to clarify our spiritual senses.

6 For at the window of my house I looked through my casement,

7 And beheld among the simple ones, I discerned among the youths, a young man void of understanding,

8 Passing through the street near her corner; and he went the way to her house,

9 In the twilight, in the evening, in the black and dark night:

10 And, behold, there met him a woman with the attire of an harlot, and subtil of heart.

11 (She is loud and stubborn; her feet abide not in her house:

12 Now is she without, now in the streets, and lieth in wait at every corner.)

13 So she caught him, and kissed him, and with an impudent face said unto him,

14 I have peace offerings with me; this day have I payed my vows.

15 Therefore came I forth to meet thee, diligently to seek thy face, and I have found thee.

*16 I have decked my bed with coverings of tapestry,
with carved works, with fine linen of Egypt.*

17 I have perfumed my bed with myrrh, aloes, and cinnamon.

*18 Come, let us take our fill of love until the morning:
let us solace ourselves with loves.*

19 For the goodman is not at home, he is gone a long journey:

*20 He hath taken a bag of money with him, and will come home
at the day appointed.*

*21 With her much fair speech she caused him to yield,
with the flattering of her lips she forced him.*

*22 He goeth after her straightway, as an ox goeth to the slaughter,
or as a fool to the correction of the stocks;*

*23 Till a dart strike through his liver; as a bird hasteth to the snare,
and knoweth not that it is for his life.*

In this story that has just been shared with us, we can see this happening in real life. Look at the multitude of young men and women showing their nakedness on the internet, in clubs, and in society. Money drives them to complete immoral and unclean deeds. Look how many people have been set up and trapped, all while they had been unaware that death was near, right at their feet. Is your life as you know it, your physical health, and your sanity worth a few minutes of rebelling against God? Wisdom would say NO! Run away, seek shelter from evil within the wings (word, wisdom, promises) of the all-mighty God who loves you and wants to bless you.

24 Hearken unto me now therefore, O ye children,
and attend to the words of my mouth.

25 Let not thine heart decline to her ways, go not astray in her paths.

26 For she hath cast down many wounded: yea,
many strong men have been slain by her.

27 Her house is the way to hell, going down to the chambers of death.

Now, to the women: just because you are a woman, don't think "good for me, I'm safe!" Don't think that the devil won't shapeshift into that immoral man that you desire. The devil uses his power to shape immoral fleshly cravings into exactly what you like, desire, and want. It is the wisdom that God used when He created the foundation of the world (Jesus Christ), that will save you from the great deceiver (the devil) through following wisdom, knowledge, understanding, and discernment granted by God.

Day 8–Proverbs Chapter Eight

1 Doth not wisdom cry? and understanding put forth her voice?

*2 She standeth in the top of high places, by the way
in the places of the paths.*

*3 She crieth at the gates, at the entry of the city,
at the coming in at the doors.*

4 Unto you, O men, I call; and my voice is to the sons of man.

*5 O ye simple, understand wisdom: and, ye fools,
be ye of an understanding heart.*

This time, King Solomon is not pleading with his child to listen to his wise teachings. Sometimes children have to hear it from someone else before they receive the message. In this chapter, wisdom is the one doing the pleading, begging us as children to use good judgment and understanding. This is important because there will come a time when failure to use wise judgment will cost us everything.

*6 Hear; for I will speak of excellent things; and the opening
of my lips shall be right things.*

*7 For my mouth shall speak truth; and wickedness
is an abomination to my lips.*

8 All the words of my mouth are in righteousness;
there is nothing froward or perverse in them.

9 They are all plain to him that understandeth,
and right to them that find knowledge.

10 Receive my instruction, and not silver; and knowledge
rather than choice gold.

11 For wisdom is better than rubies; and all the things
that may be desired are not to be compared to it.

We should definitely listen to wisdom because, in a world so corrupt, we always need a constant truth. People often focus on how to get rich quickly, but what if we focused on how to get and stay wise? Wisdom is more valuable than all the riches in the world. For wisdom is salvation.

12 I wisdom dwell with prudence, and find out knowledge
of witty inventions.

13 The fear of the Lord is to hate evil: pride, and arrogancy,
and the evil way, and the froward mouth, do I hate.

14 Counsel is mine, and sound wisdom: I am understanding;
I have strength.

15 By me kings reign, and princes decree justice.

16 By me princes rule, and nobles, even all the judges of the earth.

Good judgment, knowledge, and discernment are with wisdom. And all that fear the Lord hates evil. How many of us really hate evil?

The 1st step forward in wisdom is the fear of the Lord, and all who fear the Lord have wisdom and hate evil. We must run from evil if we want to operate in wisdom. Pride, arrogance, corruption, and perverse speech must not be found in us if we fear the Lord. Fearing God is the wisest choice we could ever make.

> *17 I love them that love me; and those that*
> *seek me early shall find me.*

> *18 Riches and honour are with me; yea, durable riches*
> *and righteousness.*

> *19 My fruit is better than gold, yea, than fine gold;*
> *and my revenue than choice silver.*

> *20 I lead in the way of righteousness, in the midst of the*
> *paths of judgment:*

> *21 That I may cause those that love me to inherit substance;*
> *and I will fill their treasures.*

This love has to be sincere. You can't say, "Oh okay, I'm just going to love wisdom just so I can inherit wealth, riches, and honor". This love cannot be one-sided or tricked. Wisdom is wise; wisdom will know you are not sincere in this counterfeit love. Wisdom is not a naive woman that can be persuaded. Remember who wisdom is and to whom wisdom belongs.

> *22 The Lord possessed me in the beginning of his way,*
> *before his works of old.*

> *23 I was set up from everlasting, from the beginning,*
> *or ever the earth was.*

24 When there were no depths, I was brought forth; when there were no fountains abounding with water.

25 Before the mountains were settled, before the hills was I brought forth:

26 While as yet he had not made the earth, nor the fields, nor the highest part of the dust of the world.

27 When he prepared the heavens, I was there: when he set a compass upon the face of the depth:

28 When he established the clouds above: when he strengthened the fountains of the deep:

29 When he gave to the sea his decree, that the waters should not pass his commandment: when he appointed the foundations of the earth:

30 Then I was by him, as one brought up with him: and I was daily his delight, rejoicing always before him;

31 Rejoicing in the habitable part of his earth; and my delights were with the sons of men.

32 Now therefore hearken unto me, O ye children: for blessed are they that keep my ways.

33 Hear instruction, and be wise, and refuse it not.

34 Blessed is the man that heareth me, watching daily at my gates, waiting at the posts of my doors.

*35 For whoso findeth me findeth life, and shall obtain
favour of the Lord.*

*36 But he that sinneth against me wrongeth his own soul:
all they that hate me love death.*

Wisdom is the spirit of Christ, our Savior, and Redeemer; who is all-knowing, all-creative, and all-restoring. This is why we should follow wisdom. If we ignore wisdom, we are rejecting Christ. The rejection of Christ is failing to love Him which results in eternal death and separation from God. But eternal life with God is the inheritance, it is the blessings, and it is the treasures that are worth more than anything in the world. Please, choose wisdom!

Day 9–Proverbs Chapter Nine

*1 Wisdom hath builded her house, she hath hewn out
her seven pillars:*

*2 She hath killed her beasts; she hath mingled her wine;
she hath also furnished her table.*

*3 She hath sent forth her maidens: she crieth upon the
highest places of the city,*

*4 Whoso is simple, let him turn in hither: as for him that wanteth
understanding, she saith to him,*

5 Come, eat of my bread, and drink of the wine which I have mingled.

6 Forsake the foolish, and live; and go in the way of understanding.

Wisdom has prepared a place for you, and all the invitations have
been sent out. Now, it is up to you to follow wisdom's instructions, use
good judgment, and get rid of simple-minded thinking.

*7 He that reproveth a scorner getteth to himself shame: and he that
rebuketh a wicked man getteth himself a blot.*

*8 Reprove not a scorner, lest he hate thee: rebuke a wise man,
and he will love thee.*

*9 Give instruction to a wise man, and he will be yet wiser:
teach a just man, and he will increase in learning.*

This is letting us know that even though you want to share wisdom with others, not everyone will receive wisdom. Many will stay in their corrupt ways rather than choose to change and live righteously. However, the wise will listen and absorb wisdom, resulting in becoming even wiser.

*10 The fear of the Lord is the beginning of wisdom: and the
knowledge of the holy is understanding.*

*11 For by me thy days shall be multiplied, and the
years of thy life shall be increased.*

*12 If thou be wise, thou shalt be wise for thyself: but if thou scornest,
thou alone shalt bear it.*

13 A foolish woman is clamorous: she is simple, and knoweth nothing.

*14 For she sitteth at the door of her house, on a seat in the
high places of the city,*

15 To call passengers who go right on their ways:

*16 Whoso is simple, let him turn in hither: and as for him that
wanteth understanding, she saith to him,*

17 Stolen waters are sweet, and bread eaten in secret is pleasant.

*18 But he knoweth not that the dead are there; and that her
guests are in the depths of hell.*

Those who are wise fear the Lord and become wiser; they will also have good judgment. When one makes good choices for themselves, it will lead to a longer life, and the benefits are beyond measure. Just as there are two sides to a coin, the opposite of wisdom is folly. Folly is to lack good sense, to be foolish, or to be blindly ignorant. Those caught in the folly's trap don't even see how close their demise truly is. They chose to stay slaves to their foolishness, entertaining themselves to death. But again, rejecting wisdom is rejecting God, and the suffering is everlasting.

Day 10–Proverbs Chapter Ten

1 The proverbs of Solomon. A wise son maketh a glad father: but a foolish son is the heaviness of his mother.

2 Treasures of wickedness profit nothing: but righteousness delivereth from death.

3 The Lord will not suffer the soul of the righteous to famish: but he casteth away the substance of the wicked.

4 He becometh poor that dealeth with a slack hand: but the hand of the diligent maketh rich.

5 He that gathereth in summer is a wise son: but he that sleepeth in harvest is a son that causeth shame.

6 Blessings are upon the head of the just: but violence covereth the mouth of the wicked.

7 The memory of the just is blessed: but the name of the wicked shall rot.

8 The wise in heart will receive commandments: but a prating fool shall fall.

9 *He that walketh uprightly walketh surely: but he that perverteth his ways shall be known.*

10 *He that winketh with the eye causeth sorrow: but a prating fool shall fall.*

11 *The mouth of a righteous man is a well of life: but violence covereth the mouth of the wicked.*

12 *Hatred stirreth up strifes: but love covereth all sins.*

13 *In the lips of him that hath understanding wisdom is found: but a rod is for the back of him that is void of understanding.*

14 *Wise men lay up knowledge: but the mouth of the foolish is near destruction.*

15 *The rich man's wealth is his strong city: the destruction of the poor is their poverty.*

16 *The labour of the righteous tendeth to life: the fruit of the wicked to sin.*

17 *He is in the way of life that keepeth instruction: but he that refuseth reproof erreth.*

18 *He that hideth hatred with lying lips, and he that uttereth a slander, is a fool.*

19 *In the multitude of words there wanteth not sin: but he that refraineth his lips is wise.*

20 *The tongue of the just is as choice silver: the heart of the wicked is little worth.*

21 *The lips of the righteous feed many: but fools die for want of wisdom.*

22 *The blessing of the Lord, it maketh rich, and he addeth no sorrow with it.*

23 *It is as sport to a fool to do mischief: but a man of understanding hath wisdom.*

24 *The fear of the wicked, it shall come upon him: but the desire of the righteous shall be granted.*

25 *As the whirlwind passeth, so is the wicked no more: but the righteous is an everlasting foundation.*

26 *As vinegar to the teeth, and as smoke to the eyes, so is the sluggard to them that send him.*

27 *The fear of the Lord prolongeth days: but the years of the wicked shall be shortened.*

28 *The hope of the righteous shall be gladness: but the expectation of the wicked shall perish.*

29 *The way of the Lord is strength to the upright: but destruction shall be to the workers of iniquity.*

30 *The righteous shall never be removed: but the wicked shall not inhabit the earth.*

31 The mouth of the just bringeth forth wisdom: but the froward tongue shall be cut out.

32 The lips of the righteous know what is acceptable: but the mouth of the wicked speaketh frowardness.

I had no choice but to leave this chapter fully intact; Solomon explained this chapter so well. This shows us that life has an either/or outcome, like a coin has two sides, heads or tails. This coin of life mirrors salvation and death; there is no meeting in the middle. You either have one or the other. Often people believe that they are not that bad, so they think that they will be okay. People often believe that being a good person will get them into Heaven, when in actuality, if you don't have Christ in your heart as your Lord and Savior, death rules over you. If wisdom does not reside in you, then you have chosen to reject God. This means you have made your bed in death's den with the wicked. There's no lukewarm with God and His wisdom; you're either hot or cold.

Each person's character reflects the master in which they serve, the God of wisdom or the god of wickedness. Wise people will show love, kindness, mercy, justice, gentleness, self-control, peace, joy, and other attributes of God. The wicked will not live in the ways of the wise. Their attributes will be hatred, violence, rudeness, corruption, selfishness, unbelief, rage, deceitfulness, and all manners of evil. Wisdom will come out of the mouths of the wise, and it takes discipline to get rid of senselessness. God will be deeply rooted in the wise by keeping and blessing them. However, those who hate wisdom will also reap what God has promised them, which is their destruction. Therefore, keep God's word, and choose wisely.

Day 11–Proverbs Chapter Eleven

1 A false balance is abomination to the Lord: but a just weight is his delight.

2 When pride cometh, then cometh shame: but with the lowly is wisdom.

3 The integrity of the upright shall guide them: but the perverseness of transgressors shall destroy them.

As we continue to learn about wisdom, we are also learning about God. We get to absorb what God likes and dislikes, as well as how His wise children operate in life. Knowing what your Master both approves and disapproves of can help you serve your Master to the best of your ability. Serving God to the best of our ability is a wise choice. In verses 1-3, we can see that God stands for honesty, justice, and humility. This means that God is just and fair in all He does, is honest and true to His word, and free from pride and arrogance for He is the Highest.

4 Riches profit not in the day of wrath: but righteousness delivereth from death.

5 The righteousness of the perfect shall direct his way: but the wicked shall fall by his own wickedness.

6 *The righteousness of the upright shall deliver them: but transgressors shall be taken in their own naughtiness.*

7 *When a wicked man dieth, his expectation shall perish: and the hope of unjust men perisheth.*

8 *The righteous is delivered out of trouble, and the wicked cometh in his stead.*

We live in a world that is driven by money. This mindset thrives on the thought that their money can save them. Their money can save them from poverty and can be of value in a state of emergency where buying supplies are necessary. Their endless amount of money can even be helpful during times of inflation. However, money cannot save you nor does it have any value during the time of God's judgment. You cannot buy your way into the presence of God, with what man has given importance to. Man attempts to give value to what God Himself has created. It is living a godly, righteous, and wise life, with the acceptance of Christ Jesus that is pleasing to God. This purchases your safety from God's judgment.

9 *An hypocrite with his mouth destroyeth his neighbour: but through knowledge shall the just be delivered.*

10 *When it goeth well with the righteous, the city rejoiceth: and when the wicked perish, there is shouting.*

11 *By the blessing of the upright the city is exalted: but it is overthrown by the mouth of the wicked.*

12 *He that is void of wisdom despiseth his neighbour: but a man of understanding holdeth his peace.*

13 *A talebearer revealeth secrets: but he that is of a faithful spirit concealeth the matter.*

14 *Where no counsel is, the people fall: but in the multitude of counsellors there is safety.*

As we develop and mature in our wisdom, our circle of friends also needs to reflect wisdom. A wise friend would not set you up for spiritual death. Their words and actions toward you will be full of life and wisdom. In the event you need to confide in your wise friend, no one else will know your business. It will be safe to share with your wise friend, as well as receive godly advice from them. However, anytime you seek counsel from a person who doesn't walk in God's wisdom, you put yourself on the path of death and destruction for foolishness leads them.

15 *He that is surety for a stranger shall smart for it: and he that hateth suretiship is sure.*

16 *A gracious woman retaineth honour: and strong men retain riches.*

17 *The merciful man doeth good to his own soul: but he that is cruel troubleth his own flesh.*

18 *The wicked worketh a deceitful work: but to him that soweth righteousness shall be a sure reward.*

19 *As righteousness tendeth to life: so he that pursueth evil pursueth it to his own death.*

20 *They that are of a froward heart are abomination to the Lord: but such as are upright in their way are his delight.*

21 Though hand join in hand, the wicked shall not be unpunished: but the seed of the righteous shall be delivered.

22 As a jewel of gold in a swine's snout, so is a fair woman which is without discretion.

23 The desire of the righteous is only good: but the expectation of the wicked is wrath.

24 There is that scattereth, and yet increaseth; and there is that withholdeth more than is meet, but it tendeth to poverty.

25 The liberal soul shall be made fat: and he that watereth shall be watered also himself.

26 He that withholdeth corn, the people shall curse him: but blessing shall be upon the head of him that selleth it.

27 He that diligently seeketh good procureth favour: but he that seeketh mischief, it shall come unto him.

28 He that trusteth in his riches shall fall; but the righteous shall flourish as a branch.

29 He that troubleth his own house shall inherit the wind: and the fool shall be servant to the wise of heart.

30 The fruit of the righteous is a tree of life; and he that winneth souls is wise.

We must take each one of these verses of Proverbs as a lesson of its own. Re-read and absorb each one, for there is true direction in every one of them. Science will tell you that for every action there is a reaction. This is Newton's third law of motion dealing with physics. Physics is defined as the natural science that studies matter, its motion and behavior through space and time as it relates to entities of energy and force. Even philosopher Pascal Wager gave strong wise counsel that it's best for a person to live as if God does exist and as you live, seek to believe in God. And if God does not exist, this logical person would have only lost or missed out on a few fleshly pleasures or experiences of the world. Whereas if God does exist and this person has NOT lived believing nor living as God exists, this person loses infinite gains on blessings, Heaven, and eternal life. Everything we do and say builds a ladder to our own personal eternal destination.

31 Behold, the righteous shall be recompensed in the earth: much more the wicked and the sinner.

Life in this world is just a test. What will we be consistent in? What will we stand for? Who are we really? For I believe that if the wicked began to see the righteous rewarded, it would be at that moment the wicked would temporarily change their ways, to receive the reward God would have for them. Once they have obtained their reward, they would turn back to who they truly are and defy God. Then God's wrath and destruction would be far greater than it will already be upon the wicked.

Day 12–Proverbs Chapter Twelve

1 Whoso loveth instruction loveth knowledge: but he that hateth reproof is brutish.

2 A good man obtaineth favour of the Lord: but a man of wicked devices will he condemn.

3 A man shall not be established by wickedness: but the root of the righteous shall not be moved.

4 A virtuous woman is a crown to her husband: but she that maketh ashamed is as rottenness in his bones.

5 The thoughts of the righteous are right: but the counsels of the wicked are deceit.

6 The words of the wicked are to lie in wait for blood: but the mouth of the upright shall deliver them.

7 The wicked are overthrown, and are not: but the house of the righteous shall stand.

8 A man shall be commended according to his wisdom: but he that is of a perverse heart shall be despised.

9 He that is despised, and hath a servant, is better than he that honoureth himself, and lacketh bread.

10 A righteous man regardeth the life of his beast: but the tender mercies of the wicked are cruel.

11 He that tilleth his land shall be satisfied with bread: but he that followeth vain persons is void of understanding.

12 The wicked desireth the net of evil men: but the root of the righteous yieldeth fruit.

13 The wicked is snared by the transgression of his lips: but the just shall come out of trouble.

14 A man shall be satisfied with good by the fruit of his mouth: and the recompence of a man's hands shall be rendered unto him.

15 The way of a fool is right in his own eyes: but he that hearkeneth unto counsel is wise.

16 A fool's wrath is presently known: but a prudent man covereth shame.

17 He that speaketh truth sheweth forth righteousness: but a false witness deceit.

18 There is that speaketh like the piercings of a sword: but the tongue of the wise is health.

19 The lip of truth shall be established for ever: but a lying tongue is but for a moment.

20 *Deceit is in the heart of them that imagine evil:*
but to the counsellors of peace is joy.

21 *There shall no evil happen to the just: but the wicked*
shall be filled with mischief.

22 *Lying lips are abomination to the Lord:*
but they that deal truly are his delight.

23 *A prudent man concealeth knowledge: but the*
heart of fools proclaimeth foolishness.

24 *The hand of the diligent shall bear rule: but the slothful*
shall be under tribute.

25 *Heaviness in the heart of man maketh it stoop:*
but a good word maketh it glad.

26 *The righteous is more excellent than his neighbour:*
but the way of the wicked seduceth them.

27 *The slothful man roasteth not that which he took in hunting:*
but the substance of a diligent man is precious.

28 *In the way of righteousness is life: and in the*
pathway thereof there is no death.

In life, we mess up, and accepting discipline with correction will keep us from making the same mistakes. These Proverbs give us the training we need to be wise. Wisdom allows us to recognize the wise from the wicked. Knowing and paying attention to these Proverbs helps us to make wise choices in every aspect of life. We have been told what will happen if we are evil. If we do not take wisdom and apply it righteously to our lives, we will not be able to use the excuse that we didn't know. We must also realize that we cannot live both righteously and immorally at the same time; the two lifestyles cannot cohabitate.

Day 13–Proverbs Chapter Thirteen

*1 A wise son heareth his father's instruction:
but a scorner heareth not rebuke.*

*2 A man shall eat good by the fruit of his mouth: but the
soul of the transgressors shall eat violence.*

*3 He that keepeth his mouth keepeth his life: but he that
openeth wide his lips shall have destruction.*

*4 The soul of the sluggard desireth, and hath nothing:
but the soul of the diligent shall be made fat.*

*5 A righteous man hateth lying: but a wicked man is loathsome,
and cometh to shame.*

*6 Righteousness keepeth him that is upright in the way:
but wickedness overthroweth the sinner.*

*7 There is that maketh himself rich, yet hath nothing:
there is that maketh himself poor, yet hath great riches.*

*8 The ransom of a man's life are his riches:
but the poor heareth not rebuke.*

9 The light of the righteous rejoiceth: but the lamp of the wicked shall be put out.

10 Only by pride cometh contention: but with the well advised is wisdom.

11 Wealth gotten by vanity shall be diminished: but he that gathereth by labour shall increase.

12 Hope deferred maketh the heart sick: but when the desire cometh, it is a tree of life.

13 Whoso despiseth the word shall be destroyed: but he that feareth the commandment shall be rewarded.

14 The law of the wise is a fountain of life, to depart from the snares of death.

15 Good understanding giveth favour: but the way of transgressors is hard.

16 Every prudent man dealeth with knowledge: but a fool layeth open his folly.

17 A wicked messenger falleth into mischief: but a faithful ambassador is health.

18 Poverty and shame shall be to him that refuseth instruction: but he that regardeth reproof shall be honoured.

As we are studying these Proverbs, for some, this will be their first time. We must see ourselves as children, children under the leadership of our parents. Now if two people began the life cycle of the world, that would make us all related. This would imply that Solomon would be our great relative speaking to us about wisdom. Therefore, we should listen and start living godly, rather than rejecting proper instruction.

Not everything is just like what it seems. We must apply wisdom to every situation, in order to know the difference between fact and fiction. The more we learn about wisdom, the more it will direct us to God. The more we know about God our Father, the more we will be able to be like Him. For we will love what He loves and despise what He despises. We must be careful not to let pride and conflict be found in us, for these are not found in God. God created some amazing things that took some time to form into maturation. So don't get caught up in things that happen too fast, for things obtained fast just don't seem to last.

19 The desire accomplished is sweet to the soul: but it is abomination to fools to depart from evil.

20 He that walketh with wise men shall be wise: but a companion of fools shall be destroyed.

21 Evil pursueth sinners: but to the righteous good shall be repayed.

22 A good man leaveth an inheritance to his children's children: and the wealth of the sinner is laid up for the just.

23 Much food is in the tillage of the poor: but there is that is destroyed for want of judgment.

24 He that spareth his rod hateth his son: but he that loveth him chasteneth him betimes.

25 *The righteous eateth to the satisfying of his soul:*
but the belly of the wicked shall want.

If you want more wisdom, hang around wise people so that wisdom will rub off on you. If you want trouble, hang out with the foolish. If you want God to give away what you have to the righteous, continue to be unrighteous. Make sure to take care of your family, so that when you depart, your children's children are cared for. This is building generational wealth. One day, God will fill His children until they are satisfied; however, God will give the wicked no satisfaction.

Day 14–Proverbs Chapter Fourteen

1 Every wise woman buildeth her house: but the foolish plucketh it down with her hands.

2 He that walketh in his uprightness feareth the Lord: but he that is perverse in his ways despiseth him.

3 In the mouth of the foolish is a rod of pride: but the lips of the wise shall preserve them.

4 Where no oxen are, the crib is clean: but much increase is by the strength of the ox.

5 A faithful witness will not lie: but a false witness will utter lies.

6 A scorner seeketh wisdom, and findeth it not: but knowledge is easy unto him that understandeth.

7 Go from the presence of a foolish man, when thou perceivest not in him the lips of knowledge.

Our Father in Heaven, holy is Your name! I ask today that You would open our spiritual eyes to Your wisdom so that we may understand both physically and spiritually. Grant Your wisdom to us in a way that is so great, that when You see us, You only see Your wisdom. Lord, let it be so!

We as a people need to take care of what God has given to us as gifts. Whatever God has blessed us with, we should be caring for it to the best of our abilities. Let's use our homes, children, spouse, businesses, etc. as examples. We should treat these blessings with love.

Only use correction and discipline for our children when necessary. Clean them up, have respect for them, feed them, nurture them, and lead them in wisdom. Do not use violence toward them or provoke them, but show them how to honor God. This is how you build your house up! As Proverbs discuss foolish behavior, the more I began to see there are foolish people in high places. Money, good looks, and status cannot hide the actions and ways of a fool. Dishonest and deceitful people are fools before God. And God will not allow them in His presence.

8 The wisdom of the prudent is to understand his way:
but the folly of fools is deceit.

9 Fools make a mock at sin: but among the righteous there is favour.

10 The heart knoweth his own bitterness; and a stranger
doth not intermeddle with his joy.

11 The house of the wicked shall be overthrown: but the
tabernacle of the upright shall flourish.

12 There is a way which seemeth right unto a man,
but the end thereof are the ways of death.

13 Even in laughter the heart is sorrowful; and the end of that mirth
is heaviness.

14 The backslider in heart shall be filled with his own ways:
and a good man shall be satisfied from himself.

15 The simple believeth every word: but the prudent man looketh well to his going.

16 A wise man feareth, and departeth from evil: but the fool rageth, and is confident.

17 He that is soon angry dealeth foolishly: and a man of wicked devices is hated.

18 The simple inherit folly: but the prudent are crowned with knowledge.

19 The evil bow before the good; and the wicked at the gates of the righteous.

20 The poor is hated even of his own neighbour: but the rich hath many friends.

21 He that despiseth his neighbour sinneth: but he that hath mercy on the poor, happy is he.

22 Do they not err that devise evil? but mercy and truth shall be to them that devise good.

23 In all labour there is profit: but the talk of the lips tendeth only to penury.

24 The crown of the wise is their riches: but the foolishness of fools is folly.

Each Proverb is so compacted with wisdom that it will be wise for you to study them more than once. That's if you truly desire wisdom from God. Each lesson within Proverbs is going to show you how to conduct yourself and how to recognize the ways of the world that are ungodly. These lessons are giving us a guide to a righteous way of living, as well as preparing us for God's eternal harvest.

25 *A true witness delivereth souls: but a deceitful witness speaketh lies.*

26 *In the fear of the Lord is strong confidence: and his children shall have a place of refuge.*

27 *The fear of the Lord is a fountain of life, to depart from the snares of death.*

28 *In the multitude of people is the king's honour: but in the want of people is the destruction of the prince.*

29 *He that is slow to wrath is of great understanding: but he that is hasty of spirit exalteth folly.*

30 *A sound heart is the life of the flesh: but envy the rottenness of the bones.*

31 *He that oppresseth the poor reproacheth his Maker: but he that honoureth him hath mercy on the poor.*

32 *The wicked is driven away in his wickedness: but the righteous hath hope in his death.*

33 *Wisdom resteth in the heart of him that hath understanding: but that which is in the midst of fools is made known.*

34 *Righteousness exalteth a nation: but sin is a reproach to any people.*

35 The king's favour is toward a wise servant: but his wrath is against him that causeth shame.

When people work hard to be rich, they don't plan on being rich for a short period of time. They usually want their wealth and riches to outlast them. There are many things that can negatively happen to you or your riches here on earth. These losses can be devastating. However, there is no devastation in God's presence. The devastation comes in when we are absent from God.

Day 15–Proverbs Chapter Fifteen

1 A soft answer turneth away wrath: but grievous words stir up anger.

2 The tongue of the wise useth knowledge aright: but the mouth of fools poureth out foolishness.

3 The eyes of the Lord are in every place, beholding the evil and the good.

4 A wholesome tongue is a tree of life: but perverseness therein is a breach in the spirit.

5 A fool despiseth his father's instruction: but he that regardeth reproof is prudent.

6 In the house of the righteous is much treasure: but in the revenues of the wicked is trouble.

7 The lips of the wise disperse knowledge: but the heart of the foolish doeth not so.

8 The sacrifice of the wicked is an abomination to the Lord: but the prayer of the upright is his delight.

9 The way of the wicked is an abomination unto the Lord: but he loveth him that followeth after righteousness.

10 *Correction is grievous unto him that forsaketh the way:*
and he that hateth reproof shall die.

Today, society believes in saying what they want to say unapologet-ically. When, in actuality, what we say and how we say it is critical when it comes to resolutions and avoiding conflict. We must remember that God has His eyes on both the just and the unjust. Now that we have the knowledge of both good and evil, it would be wise for us to bear the good fruits of the Spirit. For God detests the ways of the wicked.

11 *Hell and destruction are before the Lord: how much more*
then the hearts of the children of men?

12 *A scorner loveth not one that reproveth him:*
neither will he go unto the wise.

13 *A merry heart maketh a cheerful countenance:*
but by sorrow of the heart the spirit is broken.

14 *The heart of him that hath understanding seeketh knowledge:*
but the mouth of fools feedeth on foolishness.

15 *All the days of the afflicted are evil: but he that is*
of a merry heart hath a continual feast.

16 *Better is little with the fear of the Lord than*
great treasure and trouble therewith.

17 *Better is a dinner of herbs where love is,*
than a stalled ox and hatred therewith.

18 *A wrathful man stirreth up strife: but he that is*
slow to anger appeaseth strife.

19 The way of the slothful man is as an hedge of thorns:
but the way of the righteous is made plain.

20 A wise son maketh a glad father: but a foolish man
despiseth his mother.

21 Folly is joy to him that is destitute of wisdom:
but a man of understanding walketh uprightly.

22 Without counsel purposes are disappointed: but in the
multitude of counsellors they are established.

23 A man hath joy by the answer of his mouth: and a word
spoken in due season, how good is it!

24 The way of life is above to the wise, that he may
depart from hell beneath.

25 The Lord will destroy the house of the proud: but he will
establish the border of the widow.

26 The thoughts of the wicked are an abomination to the Lord:
but the words of the pure are pleasant words.

27 He that is greedy of gain troubleth his own house;
but he that hateth gifts shall live.

28 The heart of the righteous studieth to answer: but the
mouth of the wicked poureth out evil things.

29 The Lord is far from the wicked: but he heareth the
prayer of the righteous.

30 *The light of the eyes rejoiceth the heart: and a good report maketh the bones fat.*

31 *The ear that heareth the reproof of life abideth among the wise.*

32 *He that refuseth instruction despiseth his own soul: but he that heareth reproof getteth understanding.*

33 *The fear of the Lord is the instruction of wisdom; and before honour is humility.*

If we truly listen and follow wisdom, we will begin to mirror the attributes of God. What we value in life will begin to align itself with His will. These examples of do's and don'ts are to help guide us through life. Proverbs are repetitive, so that wisdom has a chance to stick with us. And we should overall submit to the ways of God, for He protects the wise. There is nothing wrong with being honest and pure. There is nothing wrong with rejecting evil and accepting corrections. It is the fear of the Lord that will ignite wisdom, knowledge, understanding, and discernment in our lives.

Day 16–Proverbs Chapter Sixteen

1 The preparations of the heart in man, and the answer of the tongue, is from the Lord.

2 All the ways of a man are clean in his own eyes; but the Lord weigheth the spirits.

3 Commit thy works unto the Lord, and thy thoughts shall be established.

4 The Lord hath made all things for himself: yea, even the wicked for the day of evil.

5 Every one that is proud in heart is an abomination to the Lord: though hand join in hand, he shall not be unpunished.

6 By mercy and truth iniquity is purged: and by the fear of the Lord men depart from evil.

7 When a man's ways please the Lord, he maketh even his enemies to be at peace with him.

As we continue on in Proverbs, we should be giving our plans and decisions over to God because God knows the right path for each of us. Often, we make our own plans without consulting God, and often-times His plans are quite different from our own. When we allow God to govern our decision-making, favor tends to hang around us. In a world so violent, angry, and evil, we need the almighty God on our side, making a way for us.

8 *Better is a little with righteousness than great revenues without right.*

9 *A man's heart deviseth his way: but the Lord directeth his steps.*

10 *A divine sentence is in the lips of the king: his mouth transgresseth not in judgment.*

11 *A just weight and balance are the Lord's: all the weights of the bag are his work.*

12 *It is an abomination to kings to commit wickedness: for the throne is established by righteousness.*

13 *Righteous lips are the delight of kings; and they love him that speaketh right.*

14 *The wrath of a king is as messengers of death: but a wise man will pacify it.*

15 *In the light of the king's countenance is life; and his favour is as a cloud of the latter rain.*

Scripture tells us that it is better to have a little and be with the godly than to be rich with the dishonest. I am able to see this in the lives of so many rich and famous people. Some have drug addictions that result in death from overdosing. Others commit suicide or have suicidal ideations. Many try to buy genuine love, which cannot be purchased. And others are in constant pursuit of happiness, which tends to run and hide from them. I can clearly see that this world we temporarily reside in rejects righteousness. Our justice systems and governments are not standing on fair scales when it comes to leadership. Dishonestly with one's self and others is an issue that is spreading rapidly all over the world. This is why we need to be loyal servants unto God, for in due time, He will return to restore righteousness, purpose, and order.

> *16 How much better is it to get wisdom than gold!*
> *and to get understanding rather to be chosen than silver!*

> *17 The highway of the upright is to depart from evil:*
> *he that keepeth his way preserveth his soul.*

> *18 Pride goeth before destruction, and an haughty spirit before a fall.*

> *19 Better it is to be of an humble spirit with the lowly,*
> *than to divide the spoil with the proud.*

> *20 He that handleth a matter wisely shall find good:*
> *and whoso trusteth in the Lord, happy is he.*

> *21 The wise in heart shall be called prudent: and the sweetness*
> *of the lips increaseth learning.*

> *22 Understanding is a wellspring of life unto him that hath it:*
> *but the instruction of fools is folly.*

Our world is driven by money and we can not serve both God and money. Gold and silver cannot and will not save you from the wrath of God! When our lives are changed by the word of God, we will naturally start to pull away from evil. We will feel the Holy Spirit guiding us and convicting us when we are wrong. When we follow the voice of wise guidance, it is at that moment we are on the path of wisdom.

I was conversing with a wise woman and we were discussing pride when a "WOW" revelation filled the room. Verse 18 says that pride comes before destruction. Pride was found in Lucifer before his fall. Today, many parade pride around the world, while waving a covenant sign given by God. I had to repent for rejecting the covenant sign of the rainbow. God has given it as a promise, that He would not destroy the world with water again. I had begun to reject God's covenant sign, all because humans had turned something meant for good and perverted it. God showed me that I needed not to reject Him any longer. God allowed wisdom to come in and give me understanding. The very spirit of pride found in Satan is now in the people. And the ones who pervert the rainbow are also stating what was promised by God, "fire next time". Please pay attention to wisdom. Wisdom is leading you to safety, and please whatever you do, choose wisely.

23 The heart of the wise teacheth his mouth, and addeth learning to his lips.

24 Pleasant words are as an honeycomb, sweet to the soul, and health to the bones.

25 There is a way that seemeth right unto a man, but the end thereof are the ways of death.

26 He that laboureth laboureth for himself; for his mouth craveth it of him.

27 An ungodly man diggeth up evil: and in his lips there is as a burning fire.

*28 A froward man soweth strife: and a whisperer
separateth chief friends.*

*29 A violent man enticeth his neighbour, and leadeth him
into the way that is not good.*

*30 He shutteth his eyes to devise froward things: moving his lips
he bringeth evil to pass.*

*31 The hoary head is a crown of glory, if it be found in
the way of righteousness.*

*32 He that is slow to anger is better than the mighty;
and he that ruleth his spirit than he that taketh a city.*

*33 The lot is cast into the lap; but the whole disposing
thereof is of the Lord.*

Let's be careful with our words and choose to speak wisely at all times. Let's be careful with our lives for we may be deceived by our own self-righteousness, and be on the path leading to death. When we as people are hungry for something, we work hard to satisfy ourselves. Proverbs has given us examples of wisdom in mini-lessons so that we may be aware of our surroundings. And as we are looking around, don't forget to examine ourselves through the eyes of wisdom. For we may roll the dice, but God decides where the dice land.

Day 17–Proverbs Chapter Seventeen

*1 Better is a dry morsel, and quietness therewith,
than an house full of sacrifices with strife.*

*2 A wise servant shall have rule over a son that causeth shame,
and shall have part of the inheritance among the brethren.*

*3 The fining pot is for silver, and the furnace for gold:
but the Lord trieth the hearts.*

*4 A wicked doer giveth heed to false lips; and a liar
giveth ear to a naughty tongue.*

*5 Whoso mocketh the poor reproacheth his Maker:
and he that is glad at calamities shall not be unpunished.*

*6 Children's children are the crown of old men;
and the glory of children are their fathers.*

*7 Excellent speech becometh not a fool:
much less do lying lips a prince.*

*8 A gift is as a precious stone in the eyes of him that hath it:
whithersoever it turneth, it prospereth.*

9 He that covereth a transgression seeketh love; but he that repeateth a matter separateth very friends.

10 A reproof entereth more into a wise man than an hundred stripes into a fool.

11 An evil man seeketh only rebellion: therefore a cruel messenger shall be sent against him.

12 Let a bear robbed of her whelps meet a man, rather than a fool in his folly.

13 Whoso rewardeth evil for good, evil shall not depart from his house.

14 The beginning of strife is as when one letteth out water: therefore leave off contention, before it be meddled with.

15 He that justifieth the wicked, and he that condemneth the just, even they both are abomination to the Lord.

16 Wherefore is there a price in the hand of a fool to get wisdom, seeing he hath no heart to it?

17 A friend loveth at all times, and a brother is born for adversity.

18 A man void of understanding striketh hands, and becometh surety in the presence of his friend.

19 He loveth transgression that loveth strife: and he that exalteth his gate seeketh destruction.

20 He that hath a froward heart findeth no good:
and he that hath a perverse tongue falleth into mischief.

21 He that begetteth a fool doeth it to his sorrow:
and the father of a fool hath no joy.

22 A merry heart doeth good like a medicine:
but a broken spirit drieth the bones.

23 A wicked man taketh a gift out of the bosom to
pervert the ways of judgment.

24 Wisdom is before him that hath understanding;
but the eyes of a fool are in the ends of the earth.

25 A foolish son is a grief to his father, and bitterness
to her that bare him.

26 Also to punish the just is not good, nor to strike princes for equity.

27 He that hath knowledge spareth his words:
and a man of understanding is of an excellent spirit.

28 Even a fool, when he holdeth his peace, is counted wise:
and he that shutteth his lips is esteemed a man of understanding.

After 17 days of studying wisdom, there is a plea for us to live righteously. We are being told the same things over and over again so that we can apply wisdom to our lives. Overall wisdom will be found by those who want to be wise. Take a moment to tell God, "Thank you". He has made a way for us to have wisdom and has given us the skillset to use wisdom to discern good from evil. Thank You, God, for shining Your light on the world, so that we may be able to clearly see the outcome of the path we need to take. God, I thank You that You have blessed us with wisdom, knowledge, understanding, and discernment to lead others to salvation. God, I pray for those who reject You unknowingly. I pray that You would allow Your grace and mercy to show them their faults, that they might choose salvation and live rather than experience death. Let Your will be done on earth as it is in Heaven, in Jesus' name, amen.

Day 18–Proverbs Chapter Eighteen

*1 Through desire a man, having separated himself,
seeketh and intermeddleth with all wisdom.*

*2 A fool hath no delight in understanding, but that his heart
may discover itself.*

*3 When the wicked cometh, then cometh also contempt,
and with ignominy reproach.*

*4 The words of a man's mouth are as deep waters,
and the wellspring of wisdom as a flowing brook.*

*5 It is not good to accept the person of the wicked,
to overthrow the righteous in judgment.*

6 A fool's lips enter into contention, and his mouth calleth for strokes.

*7 A fool's mouth is his destruction, and his lips are the
snare of his soul.*

*8 The words of a talebearer are as wounds, and they go down
into the innermost parts of the belly.*

*9 He also that is slothful in his work is brother to him
that is a great waster.*

If you ever really want to be able to read a person correctly, just observe them for a while. They will end up showing you their true colors; it is just a matter of time. These Proverbs are letting us know the type of people in the world and their characteristics. This must be important because our teacher is consistently repeating the information to us in hopes that we will use it wisely. Proverbs is shining a light on all characteristics and actions of people so that we won't be surprised or unaware of the fates ahead.

We are learning that there are two types of people: the ones who love God and His wisdom, and those that reject God and lean on their own understanding. You may have heard before that what we say with our mouths is so important for we are able to speak life or death to any situation. There is so much value in what we say. Speech is so important because if we take a look at the beginning of Genesis during creation, it shows us that God spoke, God said, and it was so. God designed us as men and women, created in His image and likeness, so we have been given power on this earth. Be wise with your speech, and be fair and honest with your words. Foolish people say foolish things which will lead them into terrible situations. Continue to gain wisdom, knowledge, and understanding. Use the skills that you have learned. A lazy person is one who destroys the very things that they touch.

*10 The name of the Lord is a strong tower: the righteous
runneth into it, and is safe.*

*11 The rich man's wealth is his strong city,
and as an high wall in his own conceit.*

*12 Before destruction the heart of man is haughty,
and before honour is humility.*

*13 He that answereth a matter before he heareth it,
it is folly and shame unto him.*

14 The spirit of a man will sustain his infirmity;
but a wounded spirit who can bear?

15 The heart of the prudent getteth knowledge;
and the ear of the wise seeketh knowledge.

16 A man's gift maketh room for him, and bringeth him
before great men.

17 He that is first in his own cause seemeth just;
but his neighbour cometh and searcheth him.

18 The lot causeth contentions to cease,
and parteth between the mighty.

19 A brother offended is harder to be won than a strong city:
and their contentions are like the bars of a castle.

20 A man's belly shall be satisfied with the fruit of his mouth;
and with the increase of his lips shall he be filled.

21 Death and life are in the power of the tongue: and they that love it
shall eat the fruit thereof.

22 Whoso findeth a wife findeth a good thing, and obtaineth
favour of the Lord.

23 The poor useth intreaties; but the rich answereth roughly.

24 A man that hath friends must shew himself friendly:
and there is a friend that sticketh closer than a brother.

For the name of the Lord is like a military stronghold. History has shared with us how God has done marvelous acts to show the people that He is God. And many feared the people of God because God's hand protected them. It was not until the people of God began to reject Him that God's punishment was pour out on His people. Without God's favor, grace, and mercy, nothing can save us from His destruction. In the event that your spirit feels wounded or broken, seek God the Creator, for God alone can mend all wounds and brokenness.

Stay in a position to grow in wisdom, knowledge, and understanding. Filter what you are learning, for everything that is taught doesn't always come from God. Some things only serve the purpose of evil. If you allow things to mature, they will show their true colors. There are only two paths, one to righteousness and the other to destruction. Nothing is easy about mending broken relationships. We would be much better off if we spoke to and acted right toward those we have relationships with. When a man finds a wife, he finds a treasure. Every woman is not a wife, so finding a wife is God giving favor to that man. Favor from God is a blessing beyond measure. Choose your words and actions wisely, so you can stand with the wise and be favored by God.

Day 19–Proverbs Chapter Nineteen

1 Better is the poor that walketh in his integrity, than he that is perverse in his lips, and is a fool.

2 Also, that the soul be without knowledge, it is not good; and he that hasteth with his feet sinneth.

3 The foolishness of man perverteth his way: and his heart fretteth against the Lord.

4 Wealth maketh many friends; but the poor is separated from his neighbour.

5 A false witness shall not be unpunished, and he that speaketh lies shall not escape.

6 Many will intreat the favour of the prince: and every man is a friend to him that giveth gifts.

7 All the brethren of the poor do hate him: how much more do his friends go far from him? he pursueth them with words, yet they are wanting to him.

Proverbs 19 begins with, it is better to be poor and honest than to be dishonest and a fool. Money has no value when it comes to salvation; this is why we must choose wisdom and live righteously. Be intentional with what you do and say. For in many cases, we live however we want to, and then have the nerve to blame God for the outcome of our unwise decisions. Just because someone is poor doesn't mean we should despise them. We may end up poor in something and cry out for mercy and help one day. Poor means to be lacking in necessity. Being poor isn't always monetary; you can be poor in the fruits of the spirit: love, joy, peace, patience, kindness, goodness, faithfulness, gentleness, long-suffering, and self-control.

8 He that getteth wisdom loveth his own soul: he that keepeth understanding shall find good.

9 A false witness shall not be unpunished, and he that speaketh lies shall perish.

10 Delight is not seemly for a fool; much less for a servant to have rule over princes.

11 The discretion of a man deferreth his anger; and it is his glory to pass over a transgression.

12 The king's wrath is as the roaring of a lion; but his favour is as dew upon the grass.

13 A foolish son is the calamity of his father: and the contentions of a wife are a continual dropping.

14 House and riches are the inheritance of fathers: and a prudent wife is from the Lord.

Many self-help books focus on loving yourself. Proverbs is telling us that gaining wisdom is to love yourself. This is true because if you truly love yourself, you will do whatever it takes to live and not die.

Sometimes things in life will not make sense; however, controlling your tongue and temper rewards respect. Usually, parents give good gifts to their children. Some even leave an inheritance to them such as houses and wealth for the next generation. But only God can give a wife comprehension, perception, compassion, sympathy, sensitivity, and consideration. So when you desire a great treasure that the world can not give, you must seek our Lord God in Heaven for it.

15 Slothfulness casteth into a deep sleep; and an
idle soul shall suffer hunger.

16 He that keepeth the commandment keepeth his own soul;
but he that despiseth his ways shall die.

17 He that hath pity upon the poor lendeth unto the Lord;
and that which he hath given will he pay him again.

18 Chasten thy son while there is hope, and let not
thy soul spare for his crying.

19 A man of great wrath shall suffer punishment:
for if thou deliver him, yet thou must do it again.

20 Hear counsel, and receive instruction, that thou mayest
be wise in thy latter end.

21 There are many devices in a man's heart;
nevertheless the counsel of the Lord, that shall stand.

Have you noticed that when you are up late doing nothing, you just automically want a snack? We shouldn't let idleness creep in; it's time to put an effort into wisdom. It's time that we stop playing with our soul's eternal life. So why is it so hard for us to live the way

God commands? Following God's commands places us firmly in the Lord's salvation. God says He disciplines those that He loves. So why are there so many parents unwilling to discipline their children? Don't they know that not doing so ruins their lives? Do people not know that there is a massive price to pay for being hot-tempered? But it's okay. Make your own plans, do whatever it is you want. Just remember you will be judged for everything that you do. So, get wisdom while you can, and please don't forget that God's will will be done at the end of the day.

22 The desire of a man is his kindness: and a poor man
is better than a liar.

23 The fear of the Lord tendeth to life: and he that hath it
shall abide satisfied; he shall not be visited with evil.

24 A slothful man hideth his hand in his bosom,
and will not so much as bring it to his mouth again.

25 Smite a scorner, and the simple will beware: and reprove one that
hath understanding, and he will understand knowledge.

26 He that wasteth his father, and chaseth away his mother,
is a son that causeth shame, and bringeth reproach.

27 Cease, my son, to hear the instruction that causeth to err
from the words of knowledge.

28 An ungodly witness scorneth judgment: and the
mouth of the wicked devoureth iniquity.

29 Judgments are prepared for scorners, and stripes
for the back of fools.

To the wise, this is your correction; now go be wiser. Don't stop seeking wisdom, knowledge, understanding, or discernment. To those still doing foolish things, here is your chance to stop whatever evil you are doing. Turn to God and repent so you may receive salvation. Let's not prepare our backs to be beaten as a punishment for our foolish ways.

Day 20–Proverbs Chapter Twenty

1 Wine is a mocker, strong drink is raging: and whosoever is deceived thereby is not wise.

2 The fear of a king is as the roaring of a lion: whoso provoketh him to anger sinneth against his own soul.

3 It is an honour for a man to cease from strife: but every fool will be meddling.

4 The sluggard will not plow by reason of the cold; therefore shall he beg in harvest, and have nothing.

5 Counsel in the heart of man is like deep water; but a man of understanding will draw it out.

6 Most men will proclaim every one his own goodness: but a faithful man who can find?

7 The just man walketh in his integrity: his children are blessed after him.

Wine has a way of changing a person to have no respect for others, and alcohol has a way of bringing out the worst in people. We must stay sober. Sobriety is not to keep you from having a good time. It's to keep you from ruining your own life and the lives of others. When people are under the influence, wisdom and wise decision-making leave them. And oftentimes, most people regret what they have done while they were intoxicated.

Clean yourself up with wisdom, before it is too late. When it's time for God to judge us, we want to be covered in His love, not in His raging wrath toward our evilness. These days, fighting will get you killed, so make wise choices—only the foolish engage in meaningless fighting. Work in the appropriate season so that you will be prepared for the seasons of life. As we find wisdom in God, teach your children how to live an honest and righteous life, for it's a blessing for children to follow you on the path of righteousness.

8 A king that sitteth in the throne of judgment scattereth away all evil with his eyes.

9 Who can say, I have made my heart clean, I am pure from my sin?

10 Divers weights, and divers measures, both of them are alike abomination to the Lord.

11 Even a child is known by his doings, whether his work be pure, and whether it be right.

12 The hearing ear, and the seeing eye, the Lord hath made even both of them.

13 Love not sleep, lest thou come to poverty; open thine eyes, and thou shalt be satisfied with bread.

14 It is naught, it is naught, saith the buyer: but when he is gone his way, then he boasteth.

*15 There is gold, and a multitude of rubies: but the
lips of knowledge are a precious jewel.*

*16 Take his garment that is surety for a stranger:
and take a pledge of him for a strange woman.*

*17 Bread of deceit is sweet to a man; but afterwards his mouth
shall be filled with gravel.*

*18 Every purpose is established by counsel:
and with good advice make war.*

*19 He that goeth about as a talebearer revealeth secrets:
therefore meddle not with him that flattereth with his lips.*

*20 Whoso curseth his father or his mother, his lamp shall
be put out in obscure darkness.*

*21 An inheritance may be gotten hastily at the beginning;
but the end thereof shall not be blessed.*

When God judges, you can be assured that He will use fair weights. For anything double-minded cannot stand before God. Not a double-minded person nor their thinking, rules, or ways. This is letting us know you cannot be both good and evil. One will outweigh the other and that will be the just verdict. Ears and eyes are both gifts from God; use them for His glory. Use them to make wise decisions and use them to keep away from evil. Even though evil carries a temporary pleasure, it holds on to an everlasting life of torment. Do well with what you have while you have it, and if your wisdom is not currently mature, seek God that he may grant you wisdom, knowledge, understanding, and discernment; for God is a wonderful counselor.

22 Say not thou, I will recompense evil; but wait on the Lord, and he shall save thee.

23 Divers weights are an abomination unto the Lord; and a false balance is not good.

24 Man's goings are of the Lord; how can a man then understand his own way?

25 It is a snare to the man who devoureth that which is holy, and after vows to make enquiry.

26 A wise king scattereth the wicked, and bringeth the wheel over them.

27 The spirit of man is the candle of the Lord, searching all the inward parts of the belly.

28 Mercy and truth preserve the king: and his throne is upholden by mercy.

29 The glory of young men is their strength: and the beauty of old men is the grey head.

30 The blueness of a wound cleanseth away evil: so do stripes the inward parts of the belly.

Vengeance belongs to the Lord! When we try to take matters into our own hands, we end up having evil thoughts, which can produce evil actions. Our evil actions will result in God being against us rather than for us. Talk to God about every situation that you face, whether it is good or bad. Be honest and upright in all that you do. Allow the Creator of all, our Father God in Heaven to lead our paths because He knows the future. Be careful when wagering with God, for we often do not uphold our part of the deal, whereas God will.

We need the light of God in our lives so that we will be able to see all hidden motives and intentions. We also need God to clean us up, so as loyal servants, we can, in return, show God our love and faithfulness toward Him. It's a blessing to live long and turn old and gray here on this earth. So, choose wisely while you have time.

Day 21–Proverbs Chapter Twenty-One

1 The king's heart is in the hand of the Lord, as the rivers of water: he turneth it whithersoever he will.

2 Every way of a man is right in his own eyes: but the Lord pondereth the hearts.

3 To do justice and judgment is more acceptable to the Lord than sacrifice.

4 An high look, and a proud heart, and the plowing of the wicked, is sin.

5 The thoughts of the diligent tend only to plenteousness; but of every one that is hasty only to want.

6 The getting of treasures by a lying tongue is a vanity tossed to and fro of them that seek death.

7 The robbery of the wicked shall destroy them; because they refuse to do judgment.

8 The way of man is froward and strange: but as for the pure, his work is right.

9 *It is better to dwell in a corner of the housetop, than with a brawling woman in a wide house.*

10 *The soul of the wicked desireth evil: his neighbour findeth no favour in his eyes.*

11 *When the scorner is punished, the simple is made wise: and when the wise is instructed, he receiveth knowledge.*

12 *The righteous man wisely considereth the house of the wicked: but God overthroweth the wicked for their wickedness.*

13 *Whoso stoppeth his ears at the cry of the poor, he also shall cry himself, but shall not be heard.*

14 *A gift in secret pacifieth anger: and a reward in the bosom strong wrath.*

15 *It is joy to the just to do judgment: but destruction shall be to the workers of iniquity.*

16 *The man that wandereth out of the way of understanding shall remain in the congregation of the dead.*

17 *He that loveth pleasure shall be a poor man: he that loveth wine and oil shall not be rich.*

18 *The wicked shall be a ransom for the righteous, and the transgressor for the upright.*

19 *It is better to dwell in the wilderness, than with a contentious and an angry woman.*

20 There is treasure to be desired and oil in the dwelling of the wise;
but a foolish man spendeth it up.

21 He that followeth after righteousness and mercy findeth life,
righteousness, and honour.

22 A wise man scaleth the city of the mighty, and casteth down
the strength of the confidence thereof.

23 Whoso keepeth his mouth and his tongue keepeth
his soul from troubles.

24 Proud and haughty scorner is his name,
who dealeth in proud wrath.

25 The desire of the slothful killeth him; for his hands refuse to labour.

26 He coveteth greedily all the day long: but the righteous
giveth and spareth not.

27 The sacrifice of the wicked is abomination: how much more,
when he bringeth it with a wicked mind?

28 A false witness shall perish: but the man that heareth
speaketh constantly.

29 A wicked man hardeneth his face: but as for the upright,
he directeth his way.

30 There is no wisdom nor understanding nor counsel
against the Lord.

***31** The horse is prepared against the day of battle:
but safety is of the Lord.*

Oftentimes, we think we have the power to choose who's in authority when, in fact, God puts leaders in power for the completion of His will. Remember when He hardened Pharaoh's heart? Or the time when He said, "I am raising up an evil nation to punish Israel"? Even at man's highest intellectual state of being, man cannot understand the mind of God. This is why trusting God and using our faith is so important. We must plan and prepare to do what's right at all times. Even though we have repentance for forgiveness, it's better in God's eyes if we don't need to repent because we have made the decision to live a holy and blameless life. Even the smallest things that we do that are not right are considered sins. We must correct what we see, hear, and do, for all sin is evil. You will get out what you put in, so if you want peace, you must first live peaceably.

I would like to end chapter 21 in prayer. Lord, help us to choose You this day. Lord, we ask that You direct both our spiritual and physical senses to Your will and way. God, we ask that You pour out Your holy Spirit upon us through Proverbs, so that we may live a life pleasing unto You. We ask that any strongholds that the world may have deeply rooted in our lives be released right now, in the name of Jesus. God, let Your wisdom, unmerited favor, and presence follow us for the rest of our days. In Your Son Jesus' name, amen.

Day 22–Proverbs Chapter Twenty-22

1 A good name is rather to be chosen than great riches,
and loving favour rather than silver and gold.

2 The rich and poor meet together: the Lord is the maker of them all.

3 A prudent man foreseeth the evil, and hideth himself:
but the simple pass on, and are punished.

4 By humility and the fear of the Lord are riches, and honour, and life.

5 Thorns and snares are in the way of the froward:
he that doth keep his soul shall be far from them.

6 Train up a child in the way he should go: and when he is old,
he will not depart from it.

7 The rich ruleth over the poor, and the borrower is
servant to the lender.

How we live our lives is more valuable than the riches this world has to offer. The rich and poor are alike because God created them both. Keep your eyes and ears open so that you may be aware of dangers and take the necessary steps to move wisely. Trusting in, depending on, and fearing the Lord God in Heaven has some major blessings. These blessings will follow you in this life and the next: riches, honor, and long life. Teach your children to live a righteous life pleasing to the Lord so that they may have eternal life with God. If they learn how to be wise early in life, it will stick with them when they are older.

8 He that soweth iniquity shall reap vanity: and the rod of his anger shall fail.

9 He that hath a bountiful eye shall be blessed; for he giveth of his bread to the poor.

10 Cast out the scorner, and contention shall go out; yea, strife and reproach shall cease.

11 He that loveth pureness of heart, for the grace of his lips the king shall be his friend.

12 The eyes of the Lord preserve knowledge, and he overthroweth the words of the transgressor.

13 The slothful man saith, There is a lion without, I shall be slain in the streets.

14 The mouth of strange women is a deep pit: he that is abhorred of the Lord shall fall therein.

15 Foolishness is bound in the heart of a child; but the rod of correction shall drive it far from him.

16 He that oppresseth the poor to increase his riches, and he that giveth to the rich, shall surely come to want.

Even though it seems that wicked and evil people prosper on this earth, they will surely reap what they have sown during God's time of harvest. Likewise, those who have given their life to Christ and have followed His way and truth will also reap what they have sown during the time of Harvest. Get rid of your quarrelsome behavior, mocking, and insults. Only those with a pure heart and gracious speech will have the Sovereign Ruler as a friend. Even though immaturity at a young age will bring its own set of foolishness, physical discipline will drive that foolishness far away. We need discipline and structure to keep us on the straight and narrow path. It's not easy living right for God, but, oh, is it so worth it!

17 Bow down thine ear, and hear the words of the wise,
and apply thine heart unto my knowledge.

18 For it is a pleasant thing if thou keep them within thee;
they shall withal be fitted in thy lips.

19 That thy trust may be in the Lord, I have made known
to thee this day, even to thee.

20 Have not I written to thee excellent things in
counsels and knowledge,

21 That I might make thee know the certainty of the words of truth;
that thou mightest answer the words of truth to them
that send unto thee?

22 Rob not the poor, because he is poor: neither oppress
the afflicted in the gate:

23 For the Lord will plead their cause, and spoil the soul
of those that spoiled them.

24 Make no friendship with an angry man; and with
a furious man thou shalt not go:

25 Lest thou learn his ways, and get a snare to thy soul.

26 Be not thou one of them that strike hands, or of them
that are sureties for debts.

27 If thou hast nothing to pay, why should he take away
thy bed from under thee?

28 Remove not the ancient landmark, which thy fathers have set.

29 Seest thou a man diligent in his business? he shall stand before
kings; he shall not stand before mean men.

Wisdom is calling out to us again to listen, pay attention, and obey God. Be careful how you treat the innocent, for God is their Defender. Be honest and just in all that you do. Make sure your circle mirrors the path you want to be on, or you will start to act like those in your circle. No matter what the corrupt actions are—hot-tempered, violent, thieves, deceitful, or lustful—these actions will, in return, be your actions if you are around them. Take care of your own debt because taking on someone else's debt can get you in a lot of trouble if you cannot pay. Keep working for the Lord and follow wisdom. For the King is returning soon! So please choose wisely.

Day 23–Proverbs Chapter Twenty-Three

1 When thou sittest to eat with a ruler, consider diligently what is before thee:

2 And put a knife to thy throat, if thou be a man given to appetite.

3 Be not desirous of his dainties: for they are deceitful meat.

4 Labour not to be rich: cease from thine own wisdom.

5 Wilt thou set thine eyes upon that which is not? for riches certainly make themselves wings; they fly away as an eagle toward heaven.

6 Eat thou not the bread of him that hath an evil eye, neither desire thou his dainty meats:

7 For as he thinketh in his heart, so is he: Eat and drink, saith he to thee; but his heart is not with thee.

8 The morsel which thou hast eaten shalt thou vomit up, and lose thy sweet words.

Here we are, 23 days later! How much wiser has God granted us to be by this day? I feel a wonderful peace within God's wisdom. And we still have a few more days of wisdom to cover. So, the wiser you become, the more opportunities will arise to test your wisdom and faithfulness. While you are on your journey to greatness, be careful how you conduct yourself around others, especially those who may have a bit of power and authority. Not everyone high in status is just or sent by God. We have no idea who is out to cause us harm. This is a warning to be sober and vigilant.

Restrain yourself from gluttony and embarrassment. Focus on the things in life that really matter, like producing good spiritual fruits. Focus on the things that are pleasing to God, rather than what is pleasing to society or the world. For worldly desires will all be destroyed one day. Don't surround yourself with people who are not generous because stingy people will reap poverty. Overall, don't waste your time on things that are not going to secure your place with God.

> **9** *Speak not in the ears of a fool: for he will despise the wisdom of thy words.*

> **10** *Remove not the old landmark; and enter not into the fields of the fatherless:*

> **11** *For their redeemer is mighty; he shall plead their cause with thee.*

> **12** *Apply thine heart unto instruction, and thine ears to the words of knowledge.*

> **13** *Withhold not correction from the child: for if thou beatest him with the rod, he shall not die.*

> **14** *Thou shalt beat him with the rod, and shalt deliver his soul from hell.*

> **15** *My son, if thine heart be wise, my heart shall rejoice, even mine.*

> **16** *Yea, my reins shall rejoice, when thy lips speak right things.*

Honestly, the more wisdom that God grants you, the more you would want to share that wisdom with others. However, if someone rejects wise counsel, just leave it alone. Maybe in God's timing, He will reveal His truth to them. All we can do is plant the seed of wisdom and God will do the rest. Remember to be honest in all that you do for God defends the innocent. God has a dishonest clause, that a liar will not spend any length of time in His sight. Follow the words of wisdom, and teach your children to be wise as well. A child that is properly corrected and physically disciplined has a better chance of experiencing life than death. Always remember that we must lead by example, so go out and live wisely.

> *17 Let not thine heart envy sinners: but be thou*
> *in the fear of the Lord all the day long.*

> *18 For surely there is an end; and thine expectation*
> *shall not be cut off.*

> *19 Hear thou, my son, and be wise, and guide thine heart in the way.*

> *20 Be not among winebibbers; among riotous eaters of flesh:*

> *21 For the drunkard and the glutton shall come to poverty:*
> *and drowsiness shall clothe a man with rags.*

Though society and social media continue to show us people living their lives without God, don't be persuaded away from righteousness because of what you see. God will reward those who seek and follow Him and stay on the path of righteousness. Do not fill yourself with anything of the world or its fleshly desires, for it will all lead to death and destruction.

*22 Hearken unto thy father that begat thee, and despise
not thy mother when she is old.*

*23 Buy the truth, and sell it not; also wisdom, and instruction,
and understanding.*

*24 The father of the righteous shall greatly rejoice: and he that
begetteth a wise child shall have joy of him.*

*25 Thy father and thy mother shall be glad,
and she that bare thee shall rejoice.*

26 My son, give me thine heart, and let thine eyes observe my ways.

27 For a whore is a deep ditch; and a strange woman is a narrow pit.

*28 She also lieth in wait as for a prey, and increaseth the
transgressors among men.*

Follow wise instructions from those who love you most. Other versions of the Bible say to invest in the truth and never sell it. Allow your wisdom to grow, mature, and create dividends on your behalf. If you show that you are wise, it will make those who raised you happy. Keep your eyes on God's will and on the things that are pleasing to God. Feed your soul the goodness of the Lord, and your whole being will follow suit. Any woman or man that sells their body is a trap for disaster; stay away at all costs! Any sexually unrestrained man or woman is a danger, for they plan to make others as unfaithful as they are. Don't give in to them; run from them and their unrighteous ways.

*29 Who hath woe? who hath sorrow? who hath contentions?
who hath babbling? who hath wounds without cause?
who hath redness of eyes?*

30 They that tarry long at the wine; they that go to seek mixed wine.

31 Look not thou upon the wine when it is red, when it giveth his colour in the cup, when it moveth itself aright.

32 At the last it biteth like a serpent, and stingeth like an adder.

33 Thine eyes shall behold strange women, and thine heart shall utter perverse things.

34 Yea, thou shalt be as he that lieth down in the midst of the sea, or as he that lieth upon the top of a mast.

35 They have stricken me, shalt thou say, and I was not sick; they have beaten me, and I felt it not: when shall I awake? I will seek it yet again.

Drugs and alcohol turn us away from wisdom. While we are under the influence, we tend to do things and act in ways that make God want to destroy us. When we as people operate under the influence of worldly substances we bring death to ourselves and others. We ruin the lives of the innocent. We cause fights and problems. We bring evil into the house where God is supposed to abide. We lose self-control and awareness. Is it worth it to be sick after? At risk for addiction, along with other health problems? All for a few minutes of worldly pleasure, and a lifetime of spiritual destruction? Choose to live wisely for God, for it's our only hope.

Day 24–Proverbs Chapter Twenty-Four

1 Be not thou envious against evil men, neither desire to be with them.

2 For their heart studieth destruction, and their lips talk of mischief.

3 Through wisdom is an house builded; and by understanding it is established:

4 And by knowledge shall the chambers be filled with all precious and pleasant riches.

5 A wise man is strong; yea, a man of knowledge increaseth strength.

6 For by wise counsel thou shalt make thy war: and in multitude of counsellors there is safety.

7 Wisdom is too high for a fool: he openeth not his mouth in the gate.

8 He that deviseth to do evil shall be called a mischievous person.

9 The thought of foolishness is sin: and the scorner is an abomination to men.

10 If thou faint in the day of adversity, thy strength is small.

Oftentimes, evil people appear to have the rewards that are due to the righteous. And the righteous may live lives that are not fleshly appealing to the wicked. However, it is in those very moments when we, as the wise, must not want what the wicked have nor desire their company. You, as a wise person, will not convert the wicked; however, the wicked will corrupt you. Wisdom from God is greater than any riches that this world has to offer. The world is not our home, but Heaven is our goal. Live this life wisely to be able to live forever with God.

God has a way of guiding the wise to victory. The wise are strong and mighty because God leads them. So before going into any war, be it physical or spiritual, seek wise counsel from God. Remember that wisdom is way too great for the foolish; they cannot receive God's wisdom. Don't plan to do evil, for God will not be pleased. The pressures of life will come, so strengthen yourself with the word of God so that failure won't be your outcome.

11 If thou forbear to deliver them that are drawn unto death,
and those that are ready to be slain;

12 If thou sayest, Behold, we knew it not; doth not he that pondereth
the heart consider it? and he that keepeth thy soul, doth not he know
it? and shall not he render to every man according to his works?

13 My son, eat thou honey, because it is good; and the honeycomb,
which is sweet to thy taste:

14 So shall the knowledge of wisdom be unto thy soul: when thou
hast found it, then there shall be a reward, and thy expectation
shall not be cut off.

15 Lay not wait, O wicked man, against the dwelling of the righteous;
spoil not his resting place:

16 For a just man falleth seven times, and riseth up again:
but the wicked shall fall into mischief.

Make sure that the innocent are not treated unjustly, and stand up for what is right. Don't continue your day as if you are unaware of the world's injustice. God sees all and will judge according to what they deserve. Constantly search for wisdom, for wisdom holds the fate of our future. Don't forget that wisdom is Christ. Don't disrupt or disturb the homes or the lives of the godly. One disastrous occurrence to the wicked is enough to keep them down. Though the godly may fall, they will get back up and stay in the will of God.

17 Rejoice not when thine enemy falleth, and let not
thine heart be glad when he stumbleth:

18 Lest the Lord see it, and it displease him,
and he turn away his wrath from him.

19 Fret not thyself because of evil men, neither be thou
envious at the wicked:

20 For there shall be no reward to the evil man;
the candle of the wicked shall be put out.

21 My son, fear thou the Lord and the king: and meddle not
with them that are given to change:

22 For their calamity shall rise suddenly; and who knoweth
the ruin of them both?

23 These things also belong to the wise. It is not good to have
respect of persons in judgment.

24 He that saith unto the wicked, Thou are righteous;
him shall the people curse, nations shall abhor him:

25 But to them that rebuke him shall be delight,
and a good blessing shall come upon them.

26 Every man shall kiss his lips that giveth a right answer.

27 Prepare thy work without, and make it fit for thyself in the field;
and afterwards build thine house.

28 Be not a witness against thy neighbour without cause;
and deceive not with thy lips.

29 Say not, I will do so to him as he hath done to me:
I will render to the man according to his work.

30 I went by the field of the slothful, and by the vineyard
of the man void of understanding;

31 And, lo, it was all grown over with thorns, and nettles had covered
the face thereof, and the stone wall thereof was broken down.

32 Then I saw, and considered it well: I looked upon it,
and received instruction.

33 Yet a little sleep, a little slumber, a little folding of the
hands to sleep:

34 So shall thy poverty come as one that travelleth;
and thy want as an armed man.

I just have to restate verse 17 for it is so impactful for this day and days to come. Children of God, don't be happy when your enemies are getting a taste of their own medicine, or when they are getting exactly what they deserve for their evilness. For God will then be displeased with you, and turn His anger away from them. We are not God! We are only His children. God will keep His word that all vengeance belongs to Him. Let's just stay in our lanes as humble servants to our Lord God in Heaven, and follow His instructions. Don't let those who reject God or pretend to serve Him ruffle your feathers. Remember not to be jealous of the wicked because you do not want their rewards. They have no future and God will wipe them out. Keep in mind that the fear of the Lord is the foundation of wisdom, so don't connect or identify with those who rebel against God. We have no idea what their punishment will be, when it will come, or who it will affect. So, stay with wisdom on the path of righteousness.

Day 25–Proverbs Chapter Twenty-Five

1 These are also proverbs of Solomon, which the men of Hezekiah king of Judah copied out.

2 It is the glory of God to conceal a thing: but the honour of kings is to search out a matter.

3 The heaven for height, and the earth for depth, and the heart of kings is unsearchable.

4 Take away the dross from the silver, and there shall come forth a vessel for the finer.

5 Take away the wicked from before the king, and his throne shall be established in righteousness.

6 Put not forth thyself in the presence of the king, and stand not in the place of great men:

7 For better it is that it be said unto thee, Come up hither; than that thou shouldest be put lower in the presence of the prince whom thine eyes have seen.

We have learned while studying Proverbs that we need to surround ourselves with God-given wise counsel. Those we run to for advice must run to God for advice. A descendant of King Solomon was

King Hezekiah. He was known for doing what was pleasing to God. He trusted in the Lord and there was no one like him among all the kings of Judah. We are now surrounding ourselves with wise counsel from God by researching His word. We must continue to surround ourselves with those to whom God has granted His wisdom. God chooses to hide things, and it's the leader's choice to find what is hidden.

Heavy is the head that wears the crown is a familiar saying. Leaders have a lot going on in their heads and still, our leadership cannot even map out Heaven. No matter how great the mind of leadership is, God's mind is even greater. Therefore, surround yourself with good so that good may surround you. Let the unmerited favor of God elevate you among men; don't elevate yourself lest you embarrass yourself.

8 *Go not forth hastily to strive, lest thou know not what to do in the end thereof, when thy neighbour hath put thee to shame.*

9 *Debate thy cause with thy neighbour himself; and discover not a secret to another:*

10 *Lest he that heareth it put thee to shame, and thine infamy turn not away.*

Don't be so eager to argue, prove your point, or run your mouth. It's best to gather data to have a solid case. When you are upset, be careful not to tell other people's business or secrets. You can't trust a person who has no discretion with their mouth.

11 *A word fitly spoken is like apples of gold in pictures of silver.*

12 *As an earring of gold, and an ornament of fine gold, so is a wise reprover upon an obedient ear.*

13 As the cold of snow in the time of harvest, so is a faithful mes-
senger to them that send him: for he refresheth
the soul of his masters.

14 Whoso boasteth himself of a false gift is like
clouds and wind without rain.

15 By long forbearing is a prince persuaded,
and a soft tongue breaketh the bone.

Good advice, when you need it, is just wonderful. When proper correction is given, it helps you to better yourself. It's better than shiny things of value that we as people like to show off to the world. Someone who speaks the truth is a rare find. So don't say something or make a promise you can't keep; it only brings disappointment and distrust. When the wise speak, they can deal with the worst of enemies and win without violence.

16 Hast thou found honey? eat so much as is sufficient for thee,
lest thou be filled therewith, and vomit it.

17 Withdraw thy foot from thy neighbour's house;
lest he be weary of thee, and so hate thee.

18 A man that beareth false witness against his neighbour is a maul,
and a sword, and a sharp arrow.

19 Confidence in an unfaithful man in time of trouble is like a
broken tooth, and a foot out of joint.

20 As he that taketh away a garment in cold weather, and as vinegar
upon nitre, so is he that singeth songs to an heavy heart.

21 If thine enemy be hungry, give him bread to eat; and if he be thirsty, give him water to drink:

22 For thou shalt heap coals of fire upon his head, and the Lord shall reward thee.

23 The north wind driveth away rain: so doth an angry countenance a backbiting tongue.

24 It is better to dwell in the corner of the housetop, than with a brawling woman and in a wide house.

25 As cold waters to a thirsty soul, so is good news from a far country.

26 A righteous man falling down before the wicked is as a troubled fountain, and a corrupt spring.

27 It is not good to eat much honey: so for men to search their own glory is not glory.

28 He that hath no rule over his own spirit is like a city that is broken down, and without walls.

More than likely, you have heard before that too much of a good thing can be bad for you. For example, too much honey will make you sick. Likewise, know when you have been somewhere too long and it's time to leave. For if you wear out your welcome, they wouldn't want you to come back. Keep in mind and be mindful of your words. The phrase "sticks and stones may break my bones, but words will never hurt me" is a false statement! Words hurt!!!! These Proverbs tell us that words are as harmful as being hit with an ax, being stabbed or shot! Please use your words with caution; most of those examples sound deadly. And whatever you do, don't lie, especially don't lie about someone.

While we are out here doing our best not to harm each other with our words, don't trust an unreliable person when you are in need. By doing this, you will only hurt yourself. When others are hurting, be mindful of how you try to cheer them up. You wouldn't want to break their heart which is already heavy. This next Proverb may be a bit harder to swallow. Supplying the needs of your enemy will bring them shame. Only a child of the Most High God could be so loving and kind. When you show this kind of love and kindness to your enemies, God will reward you. God's rewards are far greater than man's could ever be.

Gossiping does not show the love of God and it only brings anger, so beware of the mouth that carries all the juicy gossip. Choose wisely who you marry, for peace is better than fighting in a beautiful home. Good news is wonderful to hear and brings hope. Godly people of this generation don't give in to what evil and wicked people are doing. It will only corrupt you and hinder your reputation and salvation. Don't require others to give you glory, credit, honor, or fame. If you do, shame and embarrassment may come. And last, but not least for today, have self-control. Without self-control, anyone can take control of you. Live wisely; your life depends on it!

Day 26—Proverbs Chapter Twenty-Six

*1 As snow in summer, and as rain in harvest, so honour
is not seemly for a fool.*

*2 As the bird by wandering, as the swallow by flying,
so the curse causeless shall not come.*

*3 A whip for the horse, a bridle for the ass,
and a rod for the fool's back.*

*4 Answer not a fool according to his folly,
lest thou also be like unto him.*

*5 Answer a fool according to his folly,
lest he be wise in his own conceit.*

*6 He that sendeth a message by the hand of a fool cutteth off the feet,
and drinketh damage.*

*7 The legs of the lame are not equal: so is a parable
in the mouth of fools.*

*8 As he that bindeth a stone in a sling, so is he that
giveth honour to a fool.*

*9 As a thorn goeth up into the hand of a drunkard,
so is a parable in the mouths of fools.*

*10 The great God that formed all things both rewardeth the fool,
and rewardeth transgressors.*

11 As a dog returneth to his vomit, so a fool returneth to his folly.

*12 Seest thou a man wise in his own conceit? there is
more hope of a fool than of him.*

As we dive into Proverbs for the 26th day, we will learn the characteristics and actions, along with examples, for discerning those who are foolish and lazy. When it comes to wisdom from God, you won't find a fool with His wisdom. A fool having wisdom is an impossibility. In our times today, there are a lot of people practicing witchcraft, which the Bible tells us not to involve ourselves in. With this being said, if you wish harm to someone via a curse, if that individual does not deserve the curse, it will not come upon that person.

Just like physical discipline leads animals, a fool should be treated as such with a rod to their back. Know when to speak and not to speak with a fool, because in conversation they will bring you down to their level. If you do give wisdom to foolish people, they will think to themselves that they are wise. If you want something done or said correctly, don't send a foolish person to get the job done. If a foolish person even holds a piece of wisdom in their mouth, it would do themselves and others no good. Watch out for those who repeat their same foolishness, as well as those who think they are wise.

*13 The slothful man saith, There is a lion in the way;
a lion is in the streets.*

14 As the door turneth upon his hinges, so doth the slothful upon his bed.

15 The slothful hideth his hand in his bosom; it grieveth him to bring it again to his mouth.

16 The sluggard is wiser in his own conceit than seven men that can render a reason.

17 He that passeth by, and meddleth with strife belonging not to him, is like one that taketh a dog by the ears.

18 As a mad man who casteth firebrands, arrows, and death,

19 So is the man that deceiveth his neighbour, and saith, Am not I in sport?

20 Where no wood is, there the fire goeth out: so where there is no talebearer, the strife ceaseth.

21 As coals are to burning coals, and wood to fire; so is a contentious man to kindle strife.

22 The words of a talebearer are as wounds, and they go down into the innermost parts of the belly.

23 Burning lips and a wicked heart are like a potsherd covered with silver dross.

24 He that hateth dissembleth with his lips, and layeth up deceit within him;

25 When he speaketh fair, believe him not: for there are seven abominations in his heart.

26 Whose hatred is covered by deceit, his wickedness shall be shewed before the whole congregation.

27 Whoso diggeth a pit shall fall therein: and he that rolleth a stone, it will return upon him.

28 A lying tongue hateth those that are afflicted by it; and a flattering mouth worketh ruin.

A lazy person can only be trusted to stay at rest. Watch out for those who think they know it all, but lack substance. Stay out of other people's business and bickering. There is so much more you could be doing with your time. Lying to a friend is deadly and people do snap under pressure. Have you ever noticed that drama stops when people stop running their mouths? Or how about this: homes are safe, relationships thrive, and people are happier when rumors are nowhere to be found?

Don't be blinded by smooth words, for they might be hiding a wicked heart. Don't be deceived by sweet words. Allow God to reveal the evil heart that tries to portray itself as holy. It is only for so long that a person can pretend to be what they are not. Time and wisdom will expose their wrongdoings publicly. Treat others the way you would want to be treated. Speak the truth and tell the truth, anything else causes hate and ruin. Lifestyle choices made wisely lead to better lives.

Day 27–Proverb Chapter Twenty-Seven

1 Boast not thyself of to morrow; for thou knowest not what a day may bring forth.

2 Let another man praise thee, and not thine own mouth; a stranger, and not thine own lips.

3 A stone is heavy, and the sand weighty; but a fool's wrath is heavier than them both.

4 Wrath is cruel, and anger is outrageous; but who is able to stand before envy?

5 Open rebuke is better than secret love.

6 Faithful are the wounds of a friend; but the kisses of an enemy are deceitful.

7 The full soul loatheth an honeycomb; but to the hungry soul every bitter thing is sweet.

8 As a bird that wandereth from her nest, so is a man that wandereth from his place.

9 Ointment and perfume rejoice the heart: so doth the sweetness of a man's friend by hearty counsel.

10 Thine own friend, and thy father's friend, forsake not; neither go into thy brother's house in the day of thy calamity: for better is a neighbour that is near than a brother far off.

Now, these Proverbs are not meant to flow like a story or a pretty picture. They are meant for us to take each one and learn a full lesson from it. They are lessons to teach to our peers and for generations to come. We are to apply them to our daily lives. Each day, we should be living lives that are wise, righteous, and holy. Wisdom is a gifted treasure; if God gives it to you, use it correctly. Don't gamble with tomorrow because we have no idea what is really going to happen on that day nor can we fully control it. Allow others to tell you what a great job you are doing or how wonderful you are. Don't allow yourself to blow your own head up.

The weight of dissatisfaction created by a fool is unbearable. Jealous behavior is more dangerous than anger and wrath. When someone reprimands you openly, that experience is better than love that has been concealed from you. Getting hurt and being inflicted is better than a kiss from an enemy. Hungry people do not turn down food that is offered to them. When you get sidetracked away from home, you leave your home vulnerable to attacks. It is a very pleasant experience when a friend really means you well, and has wise advice for you. Keep your friends and friends of the family close. You just might need them quickly one day.

11 My son, be wise, and make my heart glad, that I may answer him that reproacheth me.

12 A prudent man foreseeth the evil, and hideth himself; but the simple pass on, and are punished.

13 Take his garment that is surety for a stranger, and take a pledge of him for a strange woman.

14 He that blesseth his friend with a loud voice, rising early in the morning, it shall be counted a curse to him.

15 A continual dropping in a very rainy day and a contentious woman are alike.

16 Whosoever hideth her hideth the wind, and the ointment of his right hand, which bewrayeth itself.

17 Iron sharpeneth iron; so a man sharpeneth the countenance of his friend.

18 Whoso keepeth the fig tree shall eat the fruit thereof: so he that waiteth on his master shall be honoured.

19 As in water face answereth to face, so the heart of man to man.

20 Hell and destruction are never full; so the eyes of man are never satisfied.

21 As the fining pot for silver, and the furnace for gold; so is a man to his praise.

22 Though thou shouldest bray a fool in a mortar among wheat with a pestle, yet will not his foolishness depart from him.

23 Be thou diligent to know the state of thy flocks, and look well to thy herds.

24 For riches are not for ever: and doth the crown endure to every generation?

*25 The hay appeareth, and the tender grass sheweth itself,
and herbs of the mountains are gathered.*

*26 The lambs are for thy clothing, and the goats are
the price of the field.*

*27 And thou shalt have goats' milk enough for thy food, for the food
of thy household, and for the maintenance for thy maidens.*

Wise children make their parents proud, and they're able to stick up and defend them. Be careful and take precautions to avoid danger. Others go in blindly and suffer repercussions. If you're going to allow someone else to cover another's debt, make sure you have some protection. You should collect collateral to ensure that they will keep their word. Don't startle someone in the morning; they may wake up in attack mode. A mate who likes to fight will make an annoying spouse. Trying to stop their complaints is an impossible task. Make sure you and your friends are iron material, so you will sharpen each other for greatness.

Be helpful to the ones you work for, and benefits will come from doing so. Let your heart show the real you, as clear as a reflection in the water. Some things will never be satisfied such as death, destruction, and human desire. To test the purity of precious metals, like silver and gold, requires fire. The purity of man is tested when they are being praised. One thing you cannot separate is a fool from their foolishness. Overall, you will be rewarded for your work. So, work hard and choose wisely.

Day 28–Proverbs Chapter Twenty-Eight

1 The wicked flee when no man pursueth: but the righteous are bold as a lion.

2 For the transgression of a land many are the princes thereof: but by a man of understanding and knowledge the state thereof shall be prolonged.

3 A poor man that oppresseth the poor is like a sweeping rain which leaveth no food.

4 They that forsake the law praise the wicked: but such as keep the law contend with them.

5 Evil men understand not judgment: but they that seek the Lord understand all things.

6 Better is the poor that walketh in his uprightness, than he that is perverse in his ways, though he be rich.

7 Whoso keepeth the law is a wise son: but he that is a companion of riotous men shameth his father.

8 He that by usury and unjust gain increaseth his substance, he shall gather it for him that will pity the poor.

9 *He that turneth away his ear from hearing the law,
even his prayer shall be abomination.*

10 *Whoso causeth the righteous to go astray in an evil way,
he shall fall himself into his own pit: but the upright shall
have good things in possession.*

Learning wisdom, for me, has been like mining. First, you choose what precious metal you want to look for, then you go to where you know you will find it. Because you have come this far with me, I know you desire wisdom and now, we know where to find it. The wisdom we want must be obtained from the source which is God. We have been finding these precious metals and jewels of wisdom for 28 days now. Each piece is necessary and perfect for a time that we are now being prepared for. Let's continue to gather these valuable uncut nuggets of wisdom for the journey ahead.

The wicked run away when there is nothing chasing them. The wicked will have no peace. You must sow peace to reap peace. The righteous source of strength comes from God. Let the boldness of God's magnificent power fight your battles. When you see a nation operating in stability, know that its leaders use wise counsel. Know that moral rot and chaos are not governed by wisdom. Violence and crime are high within the communities of the poor. This is why they cannot rise to change, for they tear up the very thing that could bring them a harvest of plenty. To not live according to God's will is to reject Him and worship evil. Living righteously in the sight of God is to reject and fight against evil. It makes sense for evil people not to understand justice because God is a just God. For them to understand justice would mean they would have to understand God and reject evil.

Those who are honest are close to God, and those who are dishonest are pulled away from God. The poor honest person has a better chance of receiving eternal life than a rich dishonest person. Be fair in your dealings. Using high-interest rates just to receive a profit will result in those profits being given to the ones who are kind to the poor. If you want God to hear and answer your prayers, make sure that you are a person that follows God's law. Otherwise, God will detest your prayers. If you lead good people down an evil path, you will fall into your own trap. It is those who are genuine that will receive good things from God.

11 The rich man is wise in his own conceit; but the poor that hath understanding searcheth him out.

12 When righteous men do rejoice, there is great glory: but when the wicked rise, a man is hidden.

13 He that covereth his sins shall not prosper: but whoso confesseth and forsaketh them shall have mercy.

14 Happy is the man that feareth alway: but he that hardeneth his heart shall fall into mischief.

15 As a roaring lion, and a ranging bear; so is a wicked ruler over the poor people.

16 The prince that wanteth understanding is also a great oppressor: but he that hateth covetousness shall prolong his days.

17 A man that doeth violence to the blood of any person shall flee to the pit; let no man stay him.

18 Whoso walketh uprightly shall be saved: but he that is perverse in his ways shall fall at once.

19 He that tilleth his land shall have plenty of bread: but he that followeth after vain persons shall have poverty enough.

20 *A faithful man shall abound with blessings: but he that maketh haste to be rich shall not be innocent.*

Just because a person is rich and thinks of themselves as wise doesn't mean that they are wise. When, in fact, a poor person with enough discernment can see through their trickery. To prosper, you must repent, confess, not hide your sins, and turn away from your wickedness. Those who do this will receive mercy. The fear of doing wrong is a blessing; it means the Holy Spirit is still guiding you. The wicked do not have the luxury of the Holy Spirit's guidance. Instead, they rely on their own foolishness. We need rulers who are not a danger to the poor or an oppressor to their own people. Many people are tormented by their own conscience. Wisdom tells us not to bring peace to the murderous tormented mind. We don't live in a fair or just world, so we must let God rescue, defend, and avenge us in the way He sees fit.

21 *To have respect of persons is not good: for for a piece of bread that man will transgress.*

22 *He that hasteth to be rich hath an evil eye, and considereth not that poverty shall come upon him.*

23 *He that rebuketh a man afterwards shall find more favour than he that flattereth with the tongue.*

24 *Whoso robbeth his father or his mother, and saith, It is no transgression; the same is the companion of a destroyer.*

25 *He that is of a proud heart stirreth up strife: but he that putteth his trust in the Lord shall be made fat.*

26 He that trusteth in his own heart is a fool: but whoso walketh wisely, he shall be delivered.

27 He that giveth unto the poor shall not lack: but he that hideth his eyes shall have many a curse.

28 When the wicked rise, men hide themselves: but when they perish, the righteous increase.

Do not show favoritism, for it's not right. When corrective criticism comes from a place of honesty, it is appreciated. Greed leads to fighting, whereas trusting in God leads to prosperity. Whoever gives to the poor will lack nothing while not giving to the poor brings curses. Watch what goes on in the world around you and move accordingly. Either change your ways and live righteously or remain in your sin. The choice is yours; just choose wisely.

Day 29–Proverbs Chapter Twenty-Nine

*1 He, that being often reproved hardeneth his neck,
shall suddenly be destroyed, and that without remedy.*

*2 When the righteous are in authority, the people rejoice:
but when the wicked beareth rule, the people mourn.*

*3 Whoso loveth wisdom rejoiceth his father: but he that keepeth
company with harlots spendeth his substance.*

*4 The king by judgment establisheth the land: but he that
receiveth gifts overthroweth it.*

5 A man that flattereth his neighbour spreadeth a net for his feet.

*6 In the transgression of an evil man there is a snare:
but the righteous doth sing and rejoice.*

*7 The righteous considereth the cause of the poor: but the
wicked regardeth not to know it.*

*8 Scornful men bring a city into a snare: but wise men
turn away wrath.*

*9 If a wise man contendeth with a foolish man, whether
he rage or laugh, there is no rest.*

10 The bloodthirsty hate the upright: but the just seek his soul.

11 A fool uttereth all his mind: but a wise man
keepeth it in till afterwards.

12 If a ruler hearken to lies, all his servants are wicked.

13 The poor and the deceitful man meet together:
the Lord lighteneth both their eyes.

14 The king that faithfully judgeth the poor, his throne
shall be established for ever.

15 The rod and reproof give wisdom: but a child left to himself
bringeth his mother to shame.

16 When the wicked are multiplied, transgression increaseth:
but the righteous shall see their fall.

17 Correct thy son, and he shall give thee rest; yea, he shall give
delight unto thy soul.

18 Where there is no vision, the people perish: but he that
keepeth the law, happy is he.

19 A servant will not be corrected by words: for though
he understand he will not answer.

20 Seest thou a man that is hasty in his words? there is more
hope of a fool than of him.

21 He that delicately bringeth up his servant from a child
shall have him become his son at the length.

22 An angry man stirreth up strife, and a furious man
aboundeth in transgression.

23 A man's pride shall bring him low: but honour shall
uphold the humble in spirit.

24 Whoso is partner with a thief hateth his own soul:
he heareth cursing, and bewrayeth it not.

25 The fear of man bringeth a snare: but whoso
putteth his trust in the Lord shall be safe.

26 Many seek the ruler's favour; but every man's judgment
cometh from the Lord.

27 An unjust man is an abomination to the just: and he that is upright
in the way is abomination to the wicked.

We have been reading and studying wisdom for 28 days. We should now be incorporating wisdom into our prayers. Let's use the wisdom God has given us to pray Proverbs Chapter 29 today.

Our Father God in Heaven, thank You for hearing our prayers and granting us Your wisdom. Let Your perfect wisdom correct us and place us on the path to righteousness and salvation. Help me to accept corrective criticism so that I won't be destroyed suddenly. Lord, place godly people in authority, so Your people may rejoice again. Allow me, from this day forward, to love wisdom and use my wealth wisely. Lord, our nation needs stability and freedom from bribery. Help me to keep honesty on my lips, especially toward my friends and family that their feet may be placed high above any trap that might be set out for them. Thank You, Father God, for rescuing the righteous. We, as your righteous people, shout for joy because You reveal our escape from evil traps set out for us. God, protect the rights of the poor and send resources to the right places, so that needs will be supplied and justice will be served. Lord, continue to help the wise hold back their anger and allow You to fight their battles. God, remove wicked counsel from around me. Lord, help me to discipline my children correctly and in a timely manner, so that they may be wise and bring me peace of mind. Allow me to find joy in Your word and serve You continuously. God, keep pride from being found in me and let humility flow freely within me. Lord God, I place my trust in You and Your will. Bless and keep me and my family, for all of our days. In Jesus' name, I pray, amen

Day 30–Proverbs Chapter Thirty

*1 The words of Agur the son of Jakeh, even the prophecy:
the man spake unto Ithiel, even unto Ithiel and Ucal,*

*2 Surely I am more brutish than any man, and have not the
understanding of a man.*

3 I neither learned wisdom, nor have the knowledge of the holy.

*4 Who hath ascended up into heaven, or descended? who hath
gathered the wind in his fists? who hath bound the waters in a
garment? who hath established all the ends of the earth?
what is his name, and what is his son's name, if thou canst tell?*

*5 Every word of God is pure: he is a shield unto them that
put their trust in him.*

*6 Add thou not unto his words, lest he reprove thee,
and thou be found a liar.*

7 Two things have I required of thee; deny me them not before I die:

*8 Remove far from me vanity and lies: give me neither poverty nor
riches; feed me with food convenient for me:*

9 Lest I be full, and deny thee, and say, Who is the Lord? or lest I be poor, and steal, and take the name of my God in vain.

Agur's words are here to teach us a lesson in our application of wisdom. How often do we get tired in this life? There are definitely times when we feel depressed or just way too exhausted to mentally or physically go any further. It is in those moments that we need to cry out and depend on God. In verses 2 and 3, Agur is relinquishing any claim that he himself is wise in his own eyes. He knows it is God and His Son alone who are wise. Agur places perspective on the power of God by inquiring, who but God ascends up to Heaven and back down? No physical man can do that! Who can set the boundaries or collect up the oceans but God? Who truly knows the name of the Great I am or the name of His Son, and all that He has done!? God's word is perfect and He will do, just what He said He would do, to both the just and the unjust.

The fact that Agur did not want to be a liar lets me know his desire was to be in the presence of God. His request to be neither poor nor rich speaks volumes. In either situation in his life, he did not want to be displeasing to God in any way. His desire was to be satisfied enough to place himself in positions to constantly be thankful to God for what he has; always giving God the glory for it all. Unlike Agur, we want God to bless us with all the riches of the world while keeping us from poverty as well. However, we have not taken into consideration that we might deny or insult God's holy name, as a result of being rich or poor.

10 Accuse not a servant unto his master, lest he curse thee, and thou be found guilty.

11 There is a generation that curseth their father, and doth not bless their mother.

12 There is a generation that are pure in their own eyes,
and yet is not washed from their filthiness.

13 There is a generation, O how lofty are their eyes!
and their eyelids are lifted up.

14 There is a generation, whose teeth are as swords,
and their jaw teeth as knives, to devour the poor from off the earth,
and the needy from among men.

15 The horseleach hath two daughters, crying, Give, give.
There are three things that are never satisfied, yea, four things say not,
It is enough:

16 The grave; and the barren womb; the earth that is not filled with
water; and the fire that saith not, It is enough.

17 The eye that mocketh at his father, and despiseth to obey his
mother, the ravens of the valley shall pick it out, and the
young eagles shall eat it.

18 There be three things which are too wonderful for me, yea,
four which I know not:

19 The way of an eagle in the air; the way of a serpent upon a rock;
the way of a ship in the midst of the sea;
and the way of a man with a maid.

20 Such is the way of an adulterous woman; she eateth,
and wipeth her mouth, and saith, I have done no wickedness.

Proverbs remind us to tell the truth and not lie. We are being
reminded also to follow God's commands, like honoring our father

and mother, so that we may live long and not be destroyed. We are also warned not to be evil by corrupting and devouring everything we touch along the way. We must not be like the two sucker leeches or the things in the world that will never be satisfied. God, please don't let us be like the adulterers consuming the weak, leaving only destruction without a care or worry.

*21 For three things the earth is disquieted,
and for four which it cannot bear:*

*22 For a servant when he reigneth; and a fool when he
is filled with meat;*

*23 For an odious woman when she is married;
and an handmaid that is heir to her mistress.*

*24 There be four things which are little upon the earth,
but they are exceeding wise:*

*25 The ants are a people not strong, yet they prepare
their meat in the summer;*

*26 The conies are but a feeble folk, yet make they
their houses in the rocks;*

27 The locusts have no king, yet go they forth all of them by bands;

28 The spider taketh hold with her hands, and is in kings' palaces.

29 There be three things which go well, yea, four are comely in going:

*30 A lion which is strongest among beasts,
and turneth not away for any;*

31 A greyhound; an he goat also; and a king, against whom there is no rising up.

32 If thou hast done foolishly in lifting up thyself, or if thou hast thought evil, lay thine hand upon thy mouth.

33 Surely the churning of milk bringeth forth butter, and the wringing of the nose bringeth forth blood: so the forcing of wrath bringeth forth strife.

There are so many things that occur in this life that do not appear fair and absolutely don't make any sense. How much more wisdom would God grant us over the wisdom He has given the creatures of the earth? Did He not give us dominion over them? If you have been foolish in any way, it's time to repent, turn to God, and change your ways. For if you continue to be foolish and stir up anger, a fight will occur. Today, choose wisdom and live wisely, for the Son of God will return. You should be ready!

Day 31–Proverbs Chapter Thirty-One

1 The words of king Lemuel, the prophecy that his mother taught him.

2 What, my son? and what, the son of my womb? and what, the son of my vows?

3 Give not thy strength unto women, nor thy ways to that which destroyeth kings.

4 It is not for kings, O Lemuel, it is not for kings to drink wine; nor for princes strong drink:

5 Lest they drink, and forget the law, and pervert the judgment of any of the afflicted.

6 Give strong drink unto him that is ready to perish, and wine unto those that be of heavy hearts.

7 Let him drink, and forget his poverty, and remember his misery no more.

8 Open thy mouth for the dumb in the cause of all such as are appointed to destruction.

9 Open thy mouth, judge righteously, and plead the cause of the poor and needy.

I am so glad we have made it this far, 31 days with one another. Many may have fallen off, but God has kept you right here, faithful until the end. Now we see another king was wise enough to leave us this wisdom that his mother taught him. King Lemuel had a mother full of wisdom who was set on him being righteous. Her wisdom gifted to her by God now rests with us, waiting for us to apply these principles to our lives. Over time, we should pass this wisdom to our children, both male and female, so we may raise up a generation that is pleasing unto God. King Lemuel's mother is teaching her son not to waste his time. She doesn't want her son whom people look up to for guidance, protection, leadership, and vision to be destroyed by wickedness.

Here we see that evil and wickedness come in many forms. Women can be a form of evil sent to demolish men. Not just any man; evil is after the man in charge, whose foundation is to maintain order, protect, lead, be honorable, trustworthy, and a worshiper of the Most High God. This is the man that evil desires to corrupt. If you hold any of these characteristics as a male or female, evil wants you corrupted and away from God.

Other forms of evil are in the vessels of wine and alcohol. For when mankind is drunk or under any mind-altering drug or substance, they may forget the law. In this sense, we are dealing with both the law of man, which governs the land, and the law of God, which governs your soul's salvation. Wine and alcohol have a purpose; first, alcohol is for the dying, those whose days are few because they are terminally ill. Yet, we as humans have it as a must-have at a party. Boy, do we really have things messed up today! Secondly, wine is for those who are in torment. Let the people who fall into those categories drink to forget their hardships and their troubles. But those of a royal priesthood should remain sober.

Let those who are the children of God speak up for those who cannot speak for themselves. Let the ones called by God help the helpless and poor, making sure they are treated fairly and have justice. The man with this character deserves the Proverbs 31 woman. For many years, I heard about Proverbs 31 being solely about the virtuous woman. Now we know that the man is given some directions as well in this chapter. Both males and females should be set apart from the ways of the world and live righteously before God.

10 *Who can find a virtuous woman? for her price is far above rubies.*

11 *The heart of her husband doth safely trust in her,
so that he shall have no need of spoil.*

12 *She will do him good and not evil all the days of her life.*

13 *She seeketh wool, and flax, and worketh willingly with her hands.*

14 *She is like the merchants' ships; she bringeth her food from afar.*

15 *She riseth also while it is yet night, and giveth meat to her
household, and a portion to her maidens.*

16 *She considereth a field, and buyeth it: with the fruit of her hands
she planteth a vineyard.*

17 *She girdeth her loins with strength, and strengtheneth her arms.*

18 *She perceiveth that her merchandise is good: her candle
goeth not out by night.*

19 *She layeth her hands to the spindle, and her hands hold the distaff.*

20 *She stretcheth out her hand to the poor; yea, she reacheth forth
her hands to the needy.*

21 *She is not afraid of the snow for her household: for all her household are clothed with scarlet.*

22 *She maketh herself coverings of tapestry; her clothing is silk and purple.*

23 *Her husband is known in the gates, when he sitteth among the elders of the land.*

24 *She maketh fine linen, and selleth it; and delivereth girdles unto the merchant.*

25 *Strength and honour are her clothing; and she shall rejoice in time to come.*

26 *She openeth her mouth with wisdom; and in her tongue is the law of kindness.*

27 *She looketh well to the ways of her household, and eateth not the bread of idleness.*

28 *Her children arise up, and call her blessed; her husband also, and he praiseth her.*

29 *Many daughters have done virtuously, but thou excellest them all.*

30 *Favour is deceitful, and beauty is vain: but a woman that feareth the Lord, she shall be praised.*

31 *Give her of the fruit of her hands; and let her own works praise her in the gates.*

The virtuous wife/woman is a righteous woman who is doing well as a helpmate. Her value goes way beyond worldly riches. In a world where men and women alike carry heavy loads of trust issues, her husband can trust her in every aspect. His life is improved and/or upgraded all because this righteous woman is in it. As long as she lives, she brings him satisfaction and not trauma. She plans and prepares for her household. She knows how to buy, sell, make money, and save. She works with her hands and does not mind helping others. She's prepared for the rainy days and the cold nights so that her family would be warm and well. She can do many DIY things and dresses well. In addition to her clothes, she is covered in power and respect. She is not stuck up or phony. She speaks with wisdom and corrects with kindness. She is well aware of what goes on within her home and lacks nothing because of laziness. This woman is blessed by her children. And her husband praises her by letting it be known that, there are many righteous and able women in the world but she outshines them all! In the end, the things that attract us physically do not last, but a woman who fears the Lord will be greatly praised. Husbands, openly and often praise and reward your godly virtuous wife, for all she has done and is doing...

We have made it to the end, I hope that you have decided to live boldly and righteously for God, as we mirror Christ Jesus, His Son. I am always here with you in spirit, my sisters and brothers in Christ, as we grow in God's wisdom, knowledge, understanding, and discernment. I'll be here when you are ready to repeat 31 more days in Proverbs, or when you pass this book along to another to encourage and teach them about wisdom. Go and be blessed, making wise decisions and choices until we meet in Glory. May the Holy Trinity be with you, in Jesus' name, thank God, amen.

Joy Nicole Smith